Carnegie Commission on Higher Education
Sponsored Research Studies

BETWEEN TWO WORLDS:
A PROFILE OF NEGRO HIGHER EDUCATION
Frank Bowles and Frank A. DeCosta

BREAKING THE ACCESS BARRIERS:
A PROFILE OF TWO-YEAR COLLEGES
Leland L. Medsker and Dale Tillery

ANY PERSON, ANY STUDY:
AN ESSAY ON HIGHER EDUCATION IN THE
UNITED STATES
Eric Ashby

THE NEW DEPRESSION IN HIGHER
EDUCATION:
A STUDY OF FINANCIAL CONDITIONS AT 41
COLLEGES AND UNIVERSITIES
Earl F. Cheit

FINANCING MEDICAL EDUCATION:
AN ANALYSIS OF ALTERNATIVE POLICIES
AND MECHANISMS
Rashi Fein and Gerald I. Weber

HIGHER EDUCATION IN NINE COUNTRIES:
A COMPARATIVE STUDY OF COLLEGES AND
UNIVERSITIES ABROAD
*Barbara B. Burn, Philip G. Altbach, Clark Kerr,
and James A. Perkins*

BRIDGES TO UNDERSTANDING:
INTERNATIONAL PROGRAMS OF AMERICAN
COLLEGES AND UNIVERSITIES
Irwin T. Sanders and Jennifer C. Ward

GRADUATE AND PROFESSIONAL EDUCATION,
1980:
A SURVEY OF INSTITUTIONAL PLANS
Lewis B. Mayhew

THE AMERICAN COLLEGE AND AMERICAN
CULTURE:
SOCIALIZATION AS A FUNCTION OF HIGHER
EDUCATION
Oscar Handlin and Mary F. Handlin

RECENT ALUMNI AND HIGHER EDUCATION:
A SURVEY OF COLLEGE GRADUATES
Joe L. Spaeth and Andrew M. Greeley

CHANGE IN EDUCATIONAL POLICY:
SELF-STUDIES IN SELECTED COLLEGES AND
UNIVERSITIES
Dwight R. Ladd

STATE OFFICIALS AND HIGHER EDUCATION:
A SURVEY OF THE OPINIONS AND
EXPECTATIONS OF POLICY MAKERS IN NINE
STATES
Heinz Eulau and Harold Quinley

ACADEMIC DEGREE STRUCTURES:
INNOVATIVE APPROACHES
PRINCIPLES OF REFORM IN DEGREE
STRUCTURES IN THE UNITED STATES
Stephen H. Spurr

COLLEGES OF THE FORGOTTEN AMERICANS:
A PROFILE OF STATE COLLEGES AND
REGIONAL UNIVERSITIES
E. Alden Dunham

FROM BACKWATER TO MAINSTREAM:
A PROFILE OF CATHOLIC HIGHER
EDUCATION
Andrew M. Greeley

THE ECONOMICS OF THE MAJOR PRIVATE
UNIVERSITIES
William G. Bowen
(Out of print, but available from University Microfilms.)

THE FINANCE OF HIGHER EDUCATION
Howard R. Bowen
(Out of print, but available from University Microfilms.)

ALTERNATIVE METHODS OF FEDERAL
FUNDING FOR HIGHER EDUCATION
Ron Wolk
(Out of print, but available from University Microfilms.)

INVENTORY OF CURRENT RESEARCH ON
HIGHER EDUCATION 1968
Dale M. Heckman and Warren Bryan Martin
(Out of print, but available from University Microfilms.)

*The following technical reports are available from the Carnegie Commission on Higher Education, 1947
Center Street, Berkeley, California 94704.*

RESOURCE USE IN HIGHER EDUCATION:
TRENDS IN OUTPUT AND INPUTS, 1930–1967
June O'Neill

TRENDS AND PROJECTIONS OF PHYSICIANS
IN THE UNITED STATES 1967–2002
Mark S. Blumberg

MAY 1970:
THE CAMPUS AFTERMATH OF CAMBODIA
AND KENT STATE
Richard E. Peterson and John A. Bilorusky

MENTAL ABILITY AND HIGHER EDUCATIONAL
ATTAINMENT IN THE 20TH CENTURY
Paul Taubman and Terence Wales

AMERICAN COLLEGE AND UNIVERSITY
ENROLLMENT TRENDS IN 1971
Richard E. Peterson

PAPERS ON EFFICIENCY IN THE
MANAGEMENT OF HIGHER EDUCATION
*Alexander M. Mood, Colin Bell,
Lawrence Bogard, Helen Brownlee,
and Joseph McCloskey*

The following reprints are available from the Carnegie Commission on Higher Education, 1947 Center Street, Berkeley, California 94704.

ACCELERATED PROGRAMS OF MEDICAL EDUCATION, *by Mark S. Blumberg, reprinted from* JOURNAL OF MEDICAL EDUCATION, *vol. 46, no. 8, August 1971.**

SCIENTIFIC MANPOWER FOR 1970–1985, *by Allan M. Cartter, reprinted from* SCIENCE, *vol. 172, no. 3979, pp. 132–140, April 9, 1971.*

A NEW METHOD OF MEASURING STATES' HIGHER EDUCATION BURDEN, *by Neil Timm, reprinted from* THE JOURNAL OF HIGHER EDUCATION, *vol. 42, no. 1, pp. 27–33, January 1971.**

REGENT WATCHING, *by Earl F. Cheit, reprinted from* AGB REPORTS, *vol. 13, no. 6, pp. 4–13, March 1971.*

COLLEGE GENERATIONS—FROM THE 1930s TO THE 1960s, *by Seymour M. Lipset and Everett C. Ladd, Jr., reprinted from* THE PUBLIC INTEREST, *no. 25, Summer 1971.*

AMERICAN SOCIAL SCIENTISTS AND THE GROWTH OF CAMPUS POLITICAL ACTIVISM IN THE 1960s, *by Everett C. Ladd, Jr., and Seymour M. Lipset, reprinted from* SOCIAL SCIENCES INFORMATION, *vol. 10, no. 2, April 1971.*

THE POLITICS OF AMERICAN POLITICAL SCIENTISTS, *by Everett C. Ladd, Jr., and Seymour M. Lipset, reprinted from* PS, *vol. 4, no. 2, Spring 1971.**

THE DIVIDED PROFESSORIATE, *by Seymour M. Lipset and Everett C. Ladd, Jr., reprinted from* CHANGE, *vol. 3, no. 3, pp. 54–60, May 1971.**

JEWISH ACADEMICS IN THE UNITED STATES: THEIR ACHIEVEMENTS, CULTURE AND POLITICS, *by Seymour M. Lipset and Everett C. Ladd, Jr., reprinted from* AMERICAN JEWISH YEAR BOOK, *1971.*

THE UNHOLY ALLIANCE AGAINST THE CAMPUS, *by Kenneth Keniston and Michael Lerner, reprinted from* NEW YORK TIMES MAGAZINE, *November 8, 1970 .*

PRECARIOUS PROFESSORS: NEW PATTERNS OF REPRESENTATION, *by Joseph W. Garbarino, reprinted from* INDUSTRIAL RELATIONS, *vol. 10, no. 1, February 1971.**

. . . AND WHAT PROFESSORS THINK: ABOUT STUDENT PROTEST AND MANNERS, MORALS, POLITICS, AND CHAOS ON THE CAMPUS, *by Seymour Martin Lipset and Everett C. Ladd, Jr., reprinted from* PSYCHOLOGY TODAY, *November 1970.**

DEMAND AND SUPPLY IN U.S. HIGHER EDUCATION: A PROGRESS REPORT, by Roy Radner and Leonard S. Miller, reprinted from AMERICAN ECONOMIC REVIEW, May 1970.*

RESOURCES FOR HIGHER EDUCATION: AN ECONOMIST'S VIEW, by Theodore W. Schultz, reprinted from JOURNAL OF POLITICAL ECONOMY, vol. 76, no. 3, University of Chicago, May/June 1968.*

INDUSTRIAL RELATIONS AND UNIVERSITY RELATIONS, by Clark Kerr, reprinted from PROCEEDINGS OF THE 21ST ANNUAL WINTER MEETING OF THE INDUSTRIAL RELATIONS RESEARCH ASSOCIATION, pp. 15–25.*

NEW CHALLENGES TO THE COLLEGE AND UNIVERSITY, by Clark Kerr, reprinted from Kermit Gordon (ed.), AGENDA FOR THE NATION, The Brookings Institution, Washington, D.C., 1968.*

PRESIDENTIAL DISCONTENT, by Clark Kerr, reprinted from David C. Nichols (ed.), PERSPECTIVES ON CAMPUS TENSIONS: PAPERS PREPARED FOR THE SPECIAL COMMITTEE ON CAMPUS TENSIONS, American Council on Education, Washington, D.C., September 1970.*

STUDENT PROTEST—AN INSTITUTIONAL AND NATIONAL PROFILE, by Harold Hodgkinson, reprinted from THE RECORD, vol. 71, no. 4, May 1970.*

WHAT'S BUGGING THE STUDENTS?, by Kenneth Keniston, reprinted from EDUCATIONAL RECORD, American Council on Education, Washington, D.C., Spring 1970.*

THE POLITICS OF ACADEMIA, by Seymour Martin Lipset, reprinted from David C. Nichols (ed.), PERSPECTIVES ON CAMPUS TENSIONS: PAPERS PREPARED FOR THE SPECIAL COMMITTEE ON CAMPUS TENSIONS, American Council on Education, Washington, D.C., September 1970.*

INTERNATIONAL PROGRAMS OF U.S. COLLEGES AND UNIVERSITIES: PRIORITIES FOR THE SEVENTIES, by James A. Perkins, reprinted by permission of the International Council for Educational Development, Occasional Paper no. 1, July 1971.

FACULTY UNIONISM: FROM THEORY TO PRACTICE, by Joseph W. Garbarino, reprinted from INDUSTRIAL RELATIONS, vol. 11, no. 1, pp. 1–17, February 1972.

MORE FOR LESS: HIGHER EDUCATION'S NEW PRIORITY, by Virginia B. Smith, reprinted from UNIVERSAL HIGHER EDUCATION: COSTS AND BENEFITS, American Council on Education, Washington, D.C., 1971.

ACADEMIA AND POLITICS IN AMERICA, by Seymour M. Lipset, reprinted from Thomas J. Nossiter (ed.), IMAGINATION AND PRECISION IN THE SOCIAL SCIENCES, pp. 211–289, Faber and Faber, London, 1972.

POLITICS OF ACADEMIC NATURAL SCIENTISTS AND ENGINEERS, by *Everett C. Ladd, Jr., and Seymour M. Lipset, reprinted from* SCIENCE, *vol. 176, no. 4039, pp. 1091–1100, June 9, 1972.*

THE INTELLECTUAL AS CRITIC AND REBEL: WITH SPECIAL REFERENCE TO THE UNITED STATES AND THE SOVIET UNION, by *Seymour M. Lipset and Richard B. Dobson, reprinted from* DAEDALUS, *vol. 101, no. 3, pp. 137–198, Summer 1972.*

*The Commission's stock of this reprint has been exhausted.

*The University
and the City*

The University and the City

EIGHT CASES OF INVOLVEMENT

by George Nash

with chapters by
Dan Waldorf
Robert E. Price

A Report Prepared for
The Carnegie Commission on Higher Education

MCGRAW-HILL BOOK COMPANY

New York St. Louis San Francisco Düsseldorf
London Sydney Toronto Mexico Panama
Johannesburg Kuala Lumpur Montreal
New Delhi Rio de Janeiro Singapore

The Carnegie Commission on Higher Education,
1947 Center Street, Berkeley, California 94704,
has sponsored preparation of this report as part
of a continuing effort to obtain and present
significant information for public discussion.
The views expressed are those of the authors.

THE UNIVERSITY AND THE CITY
Eight Cases of Involvement

Library of Congress Cataloging in Publication Data

Nash, George, date
The university and the city.

A report prepared for the Carnegie Commission on
Higher Education.
Includes bibliographical references.
1.   Community and college—United States.
2.   Municipal universities and colleges—United States.
I.   Carnegie Commission on Higher Education.   II.   Title.
LC238.N37   378.1'03   72-14182
ISBN 0-07-010059-4

123456789MAMM79876543

Contents

Foreword

In its report *The Campus and the City: Maximizing Assets and Reducing Liabilities,* the Carnegie Commission on Higher Education examined in detail the proposition that our colleges and universities have important roles to play in the solution of many of the problems that now face the nation's metropolitan areas. One of the most helpful sources of information for that report was a series of case studies made under the direction of Dr. George Nash. They not only provided examples of different kinds of programs undertaken by different kinds of institutions, but also discussed in useful depth some of the practical problems encountered in making such programs effective.

We are pleased to be able to play a role in making the eight case histories available to a larger audience than has heretofore had an opportunity to see it. And we want to acknowledge again our appreciation to Dr. Nash and his colleagues, Dan Waldorf and Robert E. Price, for their contributions to our own deliberations on an important concern of our time.

Clark Kerr
Chairman
Carnegie Commission
on Higher Education

February 1973

Methodology and Acknowledgments

The 8 institutions whose programs are described in this book were selected from among some 25 four-year institutions actively involved in the areas of urban, community, and minority-group problems as of 1969. They represent a cross section of types of involvement and types of institutions. They are: the University of Chicago, Illinois; Southern Illinois University, Illinois; the University of California, Los Angeles, California; Our Lady of the Lake College, Texas; Morgan State College, Maryland; Northeastern University, Massachusetts; Columbia University, New York; and Wayne State University, Michigan.

In the early fall of 1969, the president of each college or university selected agreed by letter to cooperate with the study. We began our research by gathering from each campus all available documentary materials that described the histories and substances of programs related to our research interests, as well as administrative structures impinging on institutional involvement in urban affairs.

Our field visits began in the fall of 1969 and were carried out during the succeeding year. The duration and number of visits depended on the size and complexity of the institution. Open-ended interviews—individual and group—were the principal data-collection instrument. At every campus, we talked at length to administrators, students, faculty members, and community leaders who were connected with the institution's urban program or sensitive to its evolution and substance.

The administrative details of the study and much of the data-gathering field work were done by Ann Finkelstein of the Bureau of Social Science Research. The BSSR director, Robert Bower, and staff members Albert Gollin, Helen Astin, and Mary De Carlo made useful suggestions. At several of the institutions, campus coordinators were appointed to help gather material and arrange interviews, and we are indebted to them.

Three of the case studies are authored by Dan Waldorf and Robert Price who worked with me previously at the Bureau of Applied Social Research, Columbia University, during earlier research in the area of the university and the city, which dates back to 1966. Tongsoo Song monitored the project for the U.S. Office of Education; this research was performed under contract number OEC–3–9 080798–0024 (010).

Drafts of the individual case studies in this report have been sent to the institutions for comment and review for factual error. I appreciate the assistance and attention given to the study by various college and university officials, but I assume full responsibility for the methodology, evaluations, and conclusions of each study. The views expressed are not necessarily those of the U.S. Office of Education.

George Nash

*The University
and the City*

1. *Introduction*

The combination of urban ghetto riots and student unrest on campus, both often related to university expansion in overcrowded urban settings, has caused a tremendous amount of interest to be focused on the subject of the university and the city. To illustrate how topical this interest has been we have only to note that the Newark riots were touched off by the proposed leveling of slum housing for the new campus of the New Jersey College of Medicine and Dentistry and that the Columbia student revolt was triggered by an expansion of the university into a park in Harlem.

Concern about the problems of the city launched the Urban Coalition, the Urban Institute in Washington, and Urban Observatories in a number of major cities. Each of these ventures was intended in part to make universities respond to urban problems, and a number of studies were commissioned to help point the way. It is significant that none of the organizations has lived up to its expectations and none of the studies has resulted in major publications. Universities have not been the panacea for urban problems, nor has it been easy to draw conclusions about the roles they should play.

There are reasons for these dilemmas in dealing with urban problems. First, the field of urban problems is too vast. No university could attempt to deal with even a substantial proportion of it. I will, however, offer an outline of potential areas of urban involvement. Secondly, universities and colleges were doing a great deal even before recent concern with the urban crisis arose. Thirdly, most of the problems that are defined as urban are not restricted to large cities or urban universities. Wesleyan University in Middletown, Connecticut, faces many of the same sorts of problems as New York University; but Wesleyan has done more to alleviate them. Lastly, there are inherent problems that universities face in trying to deal with urban problems. I will list the dilemmas and contradictions I have encountered.

Most universities, academicians, and scholars who try to deal with the vast urban landscape wind up specializing and concentrating on a few promising areas. My own history is a case in point. The Twentieth Century Fund asked me to write a book on the whole subject of the university and the city, but the resulting description of activity in the field was not focused enough to result in a book. I then did these eight detailed case studies of urban university involvement for the U.S. Office of Education.

Instead of attempting my original task of telling the whole urban story at each of the eight institutions, I was forced to concentrate on just one or two aspects at each school—for example, how Our Lady of the Lake, in San Antonio, Texas, was radically altered by admitting low-income Chicano girls into a program designed to prepare bilingual teachers. Instead of continuing my own work in the broad area of the university and the city I now concentrate on the areas of drug-abuse treatment, the involvement of youth in community service, and the reform of correctional facilities, with linkages to institutions of higher education in each case.

THE FOUR AREAS OF URBAN INVOLVEMENT FOR UNIVERSITIES AND COLLEGES

There are four fundamental areas in which colleges can and should be involved with urban, community, and minority-group problems. First and foremost, the college should become involved as an educator. There are five different ways in which it can do this:

1 It can become an educator of different types of people—primarily those who in the past have not met the "normal standards" for admission. The Open Admissions program of the City University of New York is an example of this.

2 It can provide a different and more relevant type of education to prepare people to live in cities and to deal with urban problems. This type of education may include student volunteer work in the community, programs that send students out into the community for part of their educational experience, and black studies programs.

3 It can provide education for public officials and technologists who will work in cities. Fels Institute at the University of Pennsylvania and the New School's Institute on New York City are in the forefront here.

4 It can provide continuing or extension education. The University of Wisconsin is a leader here.

5 It can play a role in educating paraprofessionals, new careerists, and the hard-core unemployed. Federal City College in Washington and Malcolm X College in Chicago both are very active in this area.

The second major area for involvement of colleges and universities in their communities is in their role as neighbor and citizen. Some colleges have attempted to rebuild and revitalize their neighborhoods.

The third and most traditional role of colleges and universities in dealing with the urban crisis is to provide services. Traditionally this has meant to do research.

The fourth way in which the university can deal with the urban crisis is by serving as a model or example for the rest of society.

FIFTEEN DILEMMAS AND CONTRADIC- TIONS Universities and colleges must change many of their assumptions and procedures if they are to relate to the urban crisis. I have noted 15 specific dilemmas and contradictions that confront any institution of higher education trying to become more involved in the urban crisis.

Problems related to the nature of the social sciences

1 Those universities that get the greatest allocation of research funds and have the most resources to commit to the solution of urban problems are nationally and internationally oriented and not necessarily committed to the solution of local problems.

2 Social science, which is often considered the best hope for solving a variety of urban problems, is in need of vast reform. Social scientists tend to be interested in securing grants and moving up in their departments, not in solving problems. The very nature of the research often treats those who are being studied in a demeaning fashion. Social scientists tend to write for their peers—other social scientists—not for the administrators who must solve the problems.

3 Some of the social scientists who would be the best prepared to teach about urban problems and to help the university relate to the community are not accepted in the normal social science disciplines because they have neither Ph.D.'s nor the desire to get them. Their learning has been in the real world rather than the academic world.

4 The definition of the urban field is uncertain. Most social problems exist in cities, but they also exist in rural areas. Even if the definitions of *urban problems* and *urban studies* can be agreed on, there is a lack of correlation between these terms and the academic disciplines.

Problems related to black and white relations

5 Urban problems and black problems do not necessarily encompass each other. Several universities with community service offices staffed by blacks and urban studies centers staffed by social science Ph.D.'s, who usually

happen to be white, found that there was a great deal of conflict between the two. The community service office is likely to feel that the research done by the urban studies center is not really relevant to the problems of black people. In several conferences, blacks involved in community service stated that they were not concerned about the problems of traffic movement and air pollution; they were just worried about jobs, food, and housing for black people. The white social scientists usually took offense at this and did not even attempt to reply.

6   If the president of the university picks one black man to be in charge of solving black problems at the institution, this can create problems. At some institutions the person favored in this way has caused a lot of hard feelings among others. In one case the high-ranking black who had the president's ear became a center of controversy because he blocked the promotion of other blacks. At universities that have appointed teams of black administrators, such personality problems have been avoided.

7   Just because a college institutes a number of new programs for black students and the black community does not mean that it will automatically become a good place for blacks (or, by extension, other ethnic minorities). The problem of institutional racism must be dealt with. Most predominantly white institutions of higher education have specific reputations in black academic circles. The president should be sufficiently plugged into the black academic community to find out what reputation his institution has and how to set about changing it if necessary.

Problems of funding

8   The colleges and universities that should be doing the most to help solve the urban crisis are those located in the inner parts of large cities and the predominantly black colleges. Unfortunately, many of these colleges are in extremely poor financial condition and cannot raise the resources needed to do the job. Many of the colleges and universities located in the inner cities are Catholic institutions. The majority of them operate primarily on receipts from tuition. Such an institution cannot very well charge its already hard-pressed student body more so that it can increase its involvement in urban problems. The predominantly black colleges have both serious funding problems and a shortage of adminstrative personnel. Public universities, which probably have the greatest potential for involvement in this field, are frequently located in rural settings.

9   One of the major problems of funding is a lack of continuity. Many sources of funds (e.g., the Title I program of the Higher Education Act of 1965) are willing to start programs but not to continue them. These days, when private universities and colleges are more and more strapped for funds for special programs, means of funding will have to be arranged that can be continued indefinitely. No matter how well intentioned an institution of

higher education may be, it may not be able to continue a program without a special source of funds.

Other types of dilemmas and contradictions

10   Students are a prime resource for the involvement of the university in its community. They are likely to cause problems for the university, however, both because they may be unreasonably idealistic and because they will see how the university is perceived by the community. Hence universities that have a lot of students working in the community can expect a good deal of criticism from these students.

11   The university can be seen as a cause of a number of problems and not just as a potential problem solver. While it gives to those it graduates credentials that help them get jobs, it is denying jobs to those whom it does not train. As more and more jobs require either a college degree or graduate education, the lack of such an education will be a barrier to more and more people.

12   Many institutions of higher education think that getting involved with their communities will help to improve their public relations. This is not necessarily the case. Involvement can be extremely controversial. All of the city's political chickens can come home to roost on the college campus. An involved university may have more public relations problems than an uninvolved one.

13   The extension divisions of universities potentially have the most to offer poor people in cities in need of higher education, but they have not been able to reach such people for a variety of reasons. Hence that area of the university that should be most flexible and most useful has wound up serving primarily the middle class.

14   Students from urban backgrounds who might logically be expected to become most involved in off-campus activities in cities are the least interested in such involvement. Many are first-generation college students; often they work part time while attending college; they tend to be commuters; and they are not really part of the college culture that emphasizes service. James Coleman has said that one reason today's middle-class students are dissatisfied with education is that they have already received so much education at home and through the mass media; they feel they have too much information and not enough experience. To a large extent, community involvement for middle-class students is a way of getting this first-hand experience. This is not the case for the majority of students from lower middle-class urban homes. They want a good education so that they will be able to get good jobs. This applies particularly to black students. All of the means for breaking down the walls of the classroom and getting students out into the real world for part of their education may be of relatively little interest to the typical inner-city student.

15 Each institution has a variety of constituencies that it might serve in its neighboring community. The fact that it relates well to one faction in the black community may cause it problems in trying to deal with another faction. The institution that does a good job relating to blacks may not do well relating to Puerto Ricans or poor whites. It is not really possible to serve all elements of the community equally. If the community service office is staffed by blacks, it will probably serve the black community and not other poor minorities in the same community.

POINTS OF AGREEMENT AMONG THE CASE STUDIES My original plan was to inventory and describe everything that each college or university was doing to perform these roles; however, as the field work progressed, I found that urban programs varied from institution to institution in history, content, and organization. What emerged were eight separate and highly individual stories. The focus is on *how* things got done rather than on *why,* because this approach should be more useful to practitioners looking for ways in which an institution of higher education can implement the commitment it feels to its urban environment.

Four of the institutions described in this book are public and four are private. All but Southern Illinois University are located in large cities. Each of the four types of involvement outlined above is covered, and all institutions but the University of Chicago are active as educators in their particular case studies. The first five chapters each focus on one aspect of an institution's total involvement; the last three chapters attempt to describe everything going on at the universities described.

It is as hard to generalize from the eight case studies as from the entire field. Each of the institutions pioneered, encountered difficulties, modified its methods, persevered, and met with a reasonable amount of success.

Who benefited? Just as the Peace Corps volunteers benefited as much as those they were trying to help, so these institutions were primary beneficiaries of their involvement. Each is a different and better place than it was before it attempted to respond to the problems around it.

A key element in all the case studies is leadership. Presidents or other high-ranking administrators set the goals, provided the resources and encouragement, and rewarded success. Each case study is a story revolving around personalities. At five of the institutions—Southern Illinois, UCLA, Morgan State, Northeastern, and Wayne State—the president was the crucial person. Other high-ranking administrators provided the leadership at Chicago and Our Lady of the Lake. Only at Columbia was strong leadership missing, and it is interesting to speculate how much more Columbia might have accomplished if there had been firm direction.

Each of the case studies provides numerous examples of what to do and what not to do. Each institution maintained its primary role as educator while attempting involvement in other areas. Most of the projects took longer and required more resources than they were originally expected to do. One conclusion is that an institution should choose carefully from the vast list of things it might do, so as not to dissipate its resources or disappoint those who seek its help.

2. The University of Chicago and the Woodlawn Community

One of the best-known aspects of the University of Chicago is the massive urban renewal program it has brought about. Faced with the disintegration of the neighborhood to its immediate west — Hyde Park–Kenwood — the university instigated a massive rebuilding project, which made the neighborhood a better place in which to live — except for poor blacks, most of whom were forced to move. However, some critics have complained that the rebuilding of Hyde Park–Kenwood took too little account of the wants and needs of community residents.

When the neighboring community to the east — Woodlawn — attempted to organize to improve itself, the university administration was hostile and uncooperative at first. Perhaps it was hard for university administrators to believe that such a community could do something for itself. Woodlawn is a problem-ridden, low-income black community of high density.

On the basis of this history, the present mutually beneficial relationship between the University of Chicago and The Woodlawn Organization (TWO) is surprising. Yet the seeds of today's cooperative ventures were planted during the days of distrust. The present working relationship is based on three elements:

1   A strong, popular, indigenous community organization — TWO — that combined militancy with flexibility emerged. It has grown on the basis of its success and its ability to work with the University of Chicago.

2   The strong but pragmatic administration of the university learned from its experiences in doing things the old and less satisfactory way.

3   A number of separate projects were begun by the university in the Wood-lawn area, and each has been modified under pressure from The Woodlawn Organization to serve the needs of the community better. The experiences of four university ventures — a community mental health center, a pediatric

9

medical center, a community school board, and a legal clinic — plus cooperative ventures in planning and housing have built a base on which future, more comprehensive efforts will be able to draw.

The programs cited above were started independently by various elements of the university in the mid-1960s. What drew them together into a comprehensive program was the university's work with The Woodlawn Organization (at the latter's request) to prepare its Model Cities program in 1968.

Special features of the university facilitated its response to the urban problems of The Woodlawn Organization. The University of Chicago is a fairly small (8,000 students, one-third of whom are undergraduates), private, prestigious, coeducational institution. Almost all the students attend full time, and the majority of the undergraduates live in university dormitories. There are few commuters. The university was founded in 1890 with a large grant from John D. Rockefeller. Its outstanding feature has always been academic excellence. A statement by President Edward H. Levi describes it as

an extraordinary community of extraordinary scholars. At the heart of the University is the faith of its founders in the power of the unfettered human mind. The hallmark of the University has always been its interdisciplinary nature and its faith in basic research. Faculty, students, alumni; all are the inheritors of a tradition for responsibility and the responsibility for tradition.

The university is a true *community* of scholars, with many of the faculty living in the surrounding Hyde Park–Kenwood area and walking to work. Although there is still a crime problem in the "renewed" Hyde Park–Kenwood area, and the university is forced to spend a great deal of money on its own security force, Hyde Park–Kenwood is an excellent urban place in which to live, with good housing at reasonable prices for the salaried middle class, a good deal of racial integration, and reasonable cultural amenities.

HISTORY OF UNIVERSITY-COMMUNITY RELATIONS To understand the present cooperative relationship between the University of Chicago and The Woodlawn Organization, it is necessary to know something of the history of each.

The University of Chicago's long-standing academic interest in the nation's cities traces to the Chicago School of Literature and the sociological research fostered by Robert Park and Ernest Burgess.

Chicago's research on the city, which began in the early 1920s and continues today, has been vast, including classics by Louis Wirth *(The Ghetto)*, Nels Anderson *(The Hobo)*, and Harvey Zorbaugh *(The Gold Coast and the Slum)*.

The university is located on the South Side of Chicago, which has become increasingly nonwhite in racial composition since the 1930s. Faculty members who were resident in Hyde Park–Kenwood organized the first attempt at community renewal in 1949. When their efforts faltered, the university took the lead in forming the Southeast Chicago Corporation (SECC) in 1952. It has been headed from the start by Julian Levi, a lawyer, a professor at the university, and the president's brother. Jack Meltzer, the original planner for the Southeast Chicago Corporation, was later head of the Center for Urban Studies of the University of Chicago.

The Southeast Chicago Corporation used aggressive tactics to prevent further deterioration of the Hyde Park–Kenwood area and was the sparkplug behind an urban renewal program that will eventually cost about $300 million. At the same time that it was seeking to renew its front lawn (the Hyde Park–Kenwood area), the university had decided to expand across the Midway, traditionally the boundary of its campus, into the Woodlawn area. This expansion was not welcomed by the Woodlawn community.

The Woodlawn Organization traces its origins to 1959, when clergymen of different faiths became convinced that a powerful community organization effort was needed. Under their urging, and with financial support from the Roman Catholic Archdiocese of Chicago, a coalition of community groups was formed and community organization was begun under the guidance of Saul Alinsky. Alinsky had made his reputation by successfully organizing the predominantly white Back of the Yards area of Chicago. He did not plan or direct things; instead he made it possible for the people and leaders of Woodlawn to organize and direct themselves.

Reverend Arthur Brazier, the black president of The Woodlawn Organization during many of the early years, was a match for the University's Julian Levi in aggressiveness, ability, and pragmatism. The Woodlawn Organization is a nonprofit, tax-exempt, community organization composed of more than 100 community groups— block clubs, civic groups, church groups, welfare unions, and two businessmen's associations. In Brazier's terms, TWO has been organized around a variety of issues, all related to the general goal of "providing and preserving a suitable community environment for the residents of Woodlawn. We want a place that will be good for the poor, but we don't want it to be all poor. The University would probably like Woodlawn to be similar to Hyde Park–Kenwood, but we will oppose this."

At the beginning, The Woodlawn Organization faced seemingly overwhelming problems of housing, health, education, employment, and crime; apathy on the part of the black residents of Woodlawn; and hostility from the University of Chicago.

The success of the organization can be attributed largely to the capability of the indigenous black staff and to the strategy it developed in conjunction with Alinsky's people (who pulled out as soon as the organization became viable). In operating in the community and relating to the University of Chicago, TWO developed three basic principles:

1 *Broad citizen participation* Hundreds of members of the community, men and women, old and young, serve on scores of boards and committees or are otherwise directly involved in the planning and implementation of The Woodlawn Organization's programs.

2 *Careful selection of issues* Issues were chosen for which there would be across-the-board support in the community and on which clear, measurable, and reasonably speedy victory was possible. For example, one of the first drives was against unscrupulous businessmen in the Woodlawn area. An early survey by TWO determined that residents were being overcharged, short-weighted, and sold shoddy merchandise on poor credit terms. Hundreds of area residents marched to display their displeasure and a center was set up where people could report specific complaints, which were then directed to the offending merchants. The effect was a clear-cut victory. Dishonest business practices sharply declined. The residents saw that "people power" could achieve measurable victories.

3 *Flexibility of approaches* The Woodlawn Organization developed a differentiated attitude in dealing with the University of Chicago. Because TWO was dealing with many units of the university on a variety of different problems and projects, it was inevitable that it would meet with varying degrees of success. The organization learned that it could apply pressure and express dissatisfaction with one division of the university while working smoothly with another.

The Woodlawn Organization's struggle with the university began in 1960 when the university announced plans to redevelop part of Woodlawn in much the same fashion as the Hyde Park–Kenwood area. There was a great deal of conflict, but ultimately the university was required to take the desires of the Woodlawn community into account. Eventually the university established a number of service outposts in the Woodlawn area, each planned in conjunction with The Woodlawn Organization and operated primarily for the benefit of members of the community.

The university's justification for providing services in the Woodlawn community has been that it is learning new methods for developing services in urban areas. Once these new techniques are developed, they can be applied by service organizations in other parts of the country. The university's prime functions are as an educator and a developer of knowledge, rather than as a provider of services. The Model Cities plan provided the university with the opportunity to draw up a comprehensive, reproducible program based on its first-hand experiences in the Woodlawn area.

THE MODEL CITIES PLAN The Woodlawn Organization was dissatisfied with the original Model Cities plan prepared by Mayor Daley's administration for two principal reasons:

1 There was not enough citizen participation, in either the planning or the implementation.

2 It did not offer anything that could lead to fundamental change.

A central feature of all the university services provided to Woodlawn has been citizen participation. Participation has meant that citizens of the area:

- Help to determine what is needed
- Have a say in how the services are provided
- Are employed as fully as possible in the delivery of services
- Help to evaluate the success or failure of the program by serving on advisory boards

As Arthur Brazier sees it, The Woodlawn Organization succeeded "because people in Woodlawn developed a near obsession for self-determination."

In April 1968, The Woodlawn Organization asked the university's Faculty-Woodlawn Committee to assist its own Model Cities effort. Supported by foundation money, a student team at the Center for Urban Studies began accumulating data on the Woodlawn community that would be useful in the planning process. Task forces of faculty and graduate students, many of them already involved in a colloquium and summer study project (funded by the U.S. Department of Housing and Urban Development) under the university's several demonstration programs in Woodlawn, were organized by the Center for Urban Studies to lend expert advice on problem areas selected by The Woodlawn Organization. The organization set up its own corresponding standing committees of neighborhood residents, which met with the student-faculty committees on a weekly basis. The tone of the cooperative effort was set in mid-June at a meeting in a Woodlawn church at which Julian Levi told an assembly of neighborhood residents, "You're going to decide, not the City and not the University, what kinds of solutions to Woodlawn's problems you're going to propose."

The Woodlawn Organization generated citizen participation, and the university supplied technical assistance. The university was working for the community in much the same way that a lawyer represents a client. The community chose the university to work for it, helped determine the ground rules of the relationship, and had the right to accept or reject the university's suggestions. However, since there was regular contact and feedback during the entire planning process, reciprocal education and accommodation went on continually. This made the final plan much more likely to meet the real needs of the area's residents.

The final plan that was approved by The Woodlawn Organization in November 1968 contained six areas:

1   Health
2   Social service
3   Law
4   Environmental planning and housing
5   Education
6   Economic development

Recommendations in all but the last were built around the actual experiences of programs operated in the Woodlawn area in conjunction with or without the assistance of the University of Chicago. The history of development of the university's programs in Woodlawn demonstrates how they fit into the final comprehensive Model Cities plan.

Health Woodlawn's health problems are extremely serious. The infant mortality rate—a critical index of how medically disadvantaged an area is—is 54 per 1,000. Much of the problem lies in the method of delivering health care.

The University of Chicago has undertaken at least three major innovative involvements in the field of urban health: in pediatric health care, in community mental health, and in drug-abuse treatment. We will focus on the University of Chicago's Woodlawn Child Health Center because it has encountered many of the problems that any such community-based facility will have to deal with and because it has emerged as a clear-cut success. Less has been written about it than the Community Mental Health Center and the Experimental Schools Project, but the future of those two is more uncertain. Perhaps the child-care center has had an easier time because it has not had to do battle with large established institutions such as the public school system.

The Woodlawn Child Health Center

Planning started in 1965, and in 1967 the university opened the Woodlawn Child Health Center financed by the U.S. Children's Bureau. The center is a bright, attractive, well-furnished facility, which aims to provide high-quality care with an attitude of respect for the patient. Children in the waiting room can keep busy writing on blackboards or watching a large tank of tropical fish. The inside walls are decorated with colorful posters and with pictures of the Kennedys and Martin Luther King, Jr. Relations between staff and patients and among staff members themselves are warm and friendly. The principal problem at the center is now overcrowding. It sees 1,200 children per month and has files on about 10,000 children it has seen in the first three years of its existence.

The staff of 32 is three-quarters black. One-third of the staff members live in the community. The director, John Madden, is a white pediatrician who has headed the center since it was started. Staff members appear highly motivated, pleased with their work, and extremely competent. There has been low turnover among the staff and extremely little controversy or conflict at the center, despite the innovative nature of its mission and method of operation.

A number of features allow the Woodlawn Child Health Center to deliver comprehensive services to the children of Woodlawn:

1   It has a community advisory board.

2   It is located on a main street in the community, which affords easy access.

3   It employs paraprofessionals who are primarily black residents of the local community.

4   It uses a team approach in which professionals and paraprofessionals work together on all of the child's problems.

5   A bus is used to bring handicapped or very ill children to the center and to bring those in need of more extensive care to the hospital.

6   It stresses prevention in addition to treatment. Originally prevention was to be a major goal of the center, but it is estimated that preventive care amounts to only about 20 percent of the service provided.

7   It has a university affiliation. The University of Chicago Medical School provides help in staffing with specialists, medical students, and interns and an opportunity to exchange ideas with the other university-related medical programs that are operating in Woodlawn.

The director and the advisory board   John Madden is mild-mannered, easygoing, informal, and open, but at the same time he is competent and determined. The door to his office is open, and staff members do not even knock before entering. Madden spends about half his time taking care of patients.

The community board plays a central role in planning and reviewing operations and is seen as the major way of assuring that the Child Health Center meets the real needs of Woodlawn children. Originally it was thought that the board would be composed partly of people from the community and partly of people from the university. The Woodlawn Organization insisted that six of the eleven board members be from the community. In practice all the board members have been community people, and there are no professionals on the board.

The board and the director have a good working relationship but there have been difficulties. A major problem occurred in the spring of 1970 over the dismissal of a technician whom the director viewed as disruptive. The dismissed technician told the board that he had been unfairly fired and requested that his case be reconsidered. The board decided that the dismissal should be stayed for a month while the matter was investigated. Madden told the board that if the technician were kept on, he would resign as director. The board reconsidered, and Madden stayed.

John Madden likes his work; he feels that he has accomplished something, and he wants to stay. He is extremely popular with his staff. Relations between blacks and whites at the center are excellent, and there has been no talk of replacing Madden because he is white.

The community advisory board meets monthly and was especially important in establishing the original mission of the center. The center was originally conceived as a referral center for public school teachers and nurses, board of health stations, and other agencies. The staff and board quickly realized that this buffered them from the community, was cumbersome, and further served to fragment care. It changed in the first month to accepting patients directly.

The team approach   Each patient is seen by a team consisting of a doctor, a nurse, a social worker, and a community worker. This means that, if there is rotation of staff, when a patient returns, he will still be known to several members of the team. The social worker does a write-up of the child's entire range of problems. If the family needs help with another agency, such as the welfare department or the school system, the social worker contacts the agency. The community worker visits the child's home to see how conditions there give rise to health problems.

Comprehensive care   One thing the center tires to avoid is forcing patients to go long distances for treatment. Specialists come several times a week, and the parents are now quite good about keeping appointments with them. The center also has its own x-ray and laboratory facilities, although some of the samples drawn have to be sent elsewhere for testing. Only 1 percent of those patients seen at the center are subsequently sent to hospitals.

Prevention and outreach   The community workers and the social workers have attacked a number of basic problems that give rise to poor health. They have worked to expand the free lunch program and to get food stamps. They have organized discussion groups for young mothers that focus on topics such as shopping and housekeeping in addition to child health.

The relationship of the Child Health Center to health services in the Model Cities plan   The central feature of the delivery of all services to Woodlawn, according to the Model Cities plan drawn up by The Woodlawn Organization and the University of Chicago, is a series of "pads": small centers located in storefronts and basements, each serving a two- or three-block area.

Nurses and community outreach workers would be available at the pads, and ambulance service would be on call.

There would also be a single health center, modeled loosely after the Woodlawn Child Health Center. The Model Cities plan also calls for a new method of financing health care by a compulsory health insurance program with rates based on family income.

The fit between the Model Cities plan and the Woodlawn Child Health Center model is not perfect. For example, the center's team would be broken up if the community worker is located in the pad rather than the health center. However, the experience of the Child Health Center has been of major importance in pioneering new methods, and these were drawn upon in the Model Cities plan.

The Woodlawn Mental Health Center

Development of the Chicago Board of Health–Woodlawn Mental Health Center began when two psychiatrists, Sheppard Kellam and Sheldon Schiff, decided to attempt to study and systematically deal with the mental health problems of the total community. As Schiff put it, "We wanted to develop programs with the community which would prevent the wounds rather than try to patch up these troubles later when they became more serious."

The Woodlawn Mental Health Center was the first outpost in Woodlawn operated by the University of Chicago. The need for an advisory panel was demonstrated when the co-directors got into a dispute with The Woodlawn Organization because they wanted to rent space from a white absentee landlord rather than a black businessman in the community. In response to this early crisis, a watchdog committee was appointed by The Woodlawn Organization. It later evolved into an advisory board of approximately 20 community residents that meets monthly.

Among the early involvements of the advisory board were decisions about the name of the organization and the type of furnishings that would be installed at the center. The board wanted to make sure that the name reflected the involvement of the community and not the city of Chicago. It wanted the furnishings to be durable and high in quality, to indicate the center's commitment to remain in the community.

More important, however, were the roles that The Woodlawn Organization and the advisory board played in the mission of the

Woodlawn Mental Health Center. Professionals in the area suggested that the center concentrate on the severely disturbed. Members of the community, however, were more concerned with making Woodlawn a better place to live. They stressed prevention. The community people felt that the Mental Health Center should concentrate on children and their education, especially in their early years.

The Mental Health Center has concentrated on increasing parent involvement with the schools. Some 70 percent of the children in the Woodlawn schools have had at least one parental visit to the schools each year, and 50 percent have had two or more visits. Teachers and principals have learned to relate to parents and to community people. Among the specific projects that the center and the parents have collaborated on is the picking of history texts that show black people in a more realistic light.

A key element of the program is the assignment of one community representative to every two schools. The psychiatrists themselves do not work in the schools.

Although the Woodlawn Mental Health Center achieved wide recognition and a good deal of favorable publicity, it has been extremely controversial within Woodlawn. Opponents have charged that the program attempts to force children to accommodate to a corrupt school system rather than trying to change it. Sheldon Schiff, one of the co-directors of the center, was accused of racism and forced to resign.

In part, Schiff's problems were due to his method of doing things. The Mental Health Center made extensive use of videotape and attitude surveys even though these techniques upset some (not most) community residents involved with the program. He had a tendency to lecture rather than listen, and this may have intimidated poor black people who felt intellectually inferior to any psychiatrist in the first place. He projected a stance of antagonistic skepticism, which may have been very effective in therapy, but upset the community residents who had only a brief opportunity to interact with him.

Social Service The university and the community are now working to implement some elements of the Model Cities plan. The university is readying a new building to serve as the base for coordinating an exciting new social services program financed by the state of Illinois.

The Model Cities plan drawn up by the University of Chicago and The Woodlawn Organization had three features:

1 Financial assistance is separated from services, and eligibility for financial assistance is determined easily by clear-cut criteria.

2 The plan provides for a minimum family income—$4,100 for a family of four.

3 Services are available to everyone, not only those who receive financial assistance.

When the city turned down the Model Cities plan drawn up by The Woodlawn Organization and the University of Chicago, the situation looked bleak. None of the proposed ideas was being contemplated for implementation in Woodlawn by other means. The fact that a plan had been drawn up, however, allowed the state to select the Woodlawn program as one of three demonstration projects funded by the legislature, at the rate of $3.3 million per year, as an experiment with the aim of finding ways to improve the welfare system.

The state will administer the welfare or social services program in the Woodlawn area. The approximately $1 million of state money will be used, not for financial assistance or the provision of standard services, but rather for innovative programs such as the hiring of people from the community to work with employers in developing new jobs for Woodlawn residents. Less important than the money that the state will provide is an entirely new concept of the delivery of services, which is in close agreement with the goals and procedures outlined in the Model Cities plan. The $4,100 minimum income for a family of four will not be part of the program.

Law For several years the University of Chicago Law School has operated the Edwin F. Mandel Clinic in conjunction with the Legal Aid Bureau. Active in the clinic have been 50 students from the Law School, faculty members of the Law School, and a panel of 25 consulting attorneys who participate in the economic development and test case components of the clinic's practice. Approximately 100 people visit the clinic each week with legal problems in the areas of housing, consumer credit, domestic matters, welfare, and juvenile and criminal law. Although many of the clients require only advice or minimal representation (a letter or a telephone call), approximately 25 percent of the cases involve extensive representation or litigation. The Law School and the clinic have attempted to engage in preventive law and community legal education through a series of articles in The Woodlawn Organization newspaper, *The Observer,* and by conducting forums on tenants' rights, the rights of citizens on the street, and other legal matters.

Those who drew up the Model Cities legal program realized that the Edwin F. Mandel Clinic suffered from a number of deficiencies in attempting to satisfy the legal needs of the community. First, because the clinic was not community operated, many residents regard it with suspicion. Secondly, many Woodlawn residents consult an attorney only after a legal problem has reached the acute stage.

The Model Cities plan restricted the Edwin F. Mandel Clinic to trial and test cases that would seek to clarify and expand the rights of Woodlawn residents and to train community lay advocates to be paraprofessionals in the legal field. The plan also called for formation of a number of new legal services, such as a neighborhood law firm, a dispute service, and a youth advisory section to handle juvenile legal problems.

Environmental Planning and Housing

In the opinion of The Woodlawn Organization, the major problem in the community is substandard housing. The Woodlawn Organization long ago went on record that it wanted new housing to provide an economic mix, allowing middle-income people to move into the neighborhood. New housing was to escape the institutional stigma that characterizes much of the high-rise public housing built in Chicago. The University of Chicago and The Woodlawn Organization have collaborated on several housing ventures.

It was the university's plan to build its new South Campus in Woodlawn, with the aid of Urban Renewal, that first brought the university and The Woodlawn Organization into conflict. Under a complex federal urban renewal formula the University of Chicago had accumulated credits that the city of Chicago could use in lieu of the cash contribution required from it for proposed urban renewal in the Woodlawn area. However, the university wanted assurance that it would be given the chance to buy some of the proposed urban renewal land for expansion of its South Campus. The Woodlawn Organization refused to go along with the plan until its members were assured that some benefit would come to the black Woodlawn community.

A deadlock ensued, with a great deal of bitterness on both sides; it was broken by Mayor Daley personally in 1963. The major points of the agreement were that:

1   A citizens' committee would be appointed by the mayor to deal with urban renewal in Woodlawn, and The Woodlawn Organization would have a majority of the members.

2   An area of deteriorated commercial structures would be cleared for low-rise, low-cost (but not public) housing.

3   No buildings at the projected South Campus location would be demolished until construction of this housing was actually under way.

The result is Woodlawn Gardens, a 26-building, 500-apartment complex. Rents range from $99 a month for an efficiency apartment to $160 for a three-bedroom duplex. Preference in renting is given to those who have previously been displaced by urban renewal. One-fifth of the apartments are subsidized by the rent-supplement plan. Although the apartments are all occupied and there is a long waiting list, relatively few very poor people have been able to move in. The housing was built with federal financing, but The Woodlawn Organization needed other financial help to plan and oversee construction of the buildings. The Kate Maremont Foundation provided seed money for the program on the condition that it be returned when the housing was completed.

The University of Chicago had originally planned to use part of its urban renewal land in the Woodlawn area for the construction of a veterans' hospital, which it hoped would be a major employer of Woodlawn residents. The site for the hospital was shifted and the university has now leased the land to The Woodlawn Organization for housing. The university is making temporary loans to TWO not to exceed $500,000, to be used to secure architectural, legal, and other necessary services that are prerequisites for full federal financing of this housing program. The university is also working with The Woodlawn Organization to help it secure financing for additional housing.

Another area in which the university has become involved is that of relocating people who are forced to move as a result of the new South Campus buildings. The number of families who need help beyond that normally provided is small, but unless special provisions had been made, they would have suffered serious problems.

The university made available $15,000 to meet the needs of people with three specific types of problems:

1   Some people had once lived in public housing and had moved out owing rent. They wanted to get back in but could not do so unless they cleared their balances.

2   There were people who wanted to buy houses and did not have enough money for the whole down payment.

3   Some people who had lived on the site had been moved away. Their moving expenses had been paid at that point. They now wanted to move back into the new housing and had no way of financing the second move.

The Model Cities plan for improving the environment and providing housing called for a comprehensive program aimed at improving the whole community and serving the needs of the people. The Model Cities plan recognized that improvements in housing and environment alone were not sufficient for community renewal; development of a sense of community and provision of adequate services were also essential.

Education   The Woodlawn Experimental School District operated ten schools (seven primary, two junior high, and one senior high) as experimental schools with supplementary funding from Title III of the Elementary and Secondary Education Act under a program that ended in June 1971. Key elements of the program were the Woodlawn Community Board, composed of 21 members (7 each appointed by The Woodlawn Organization, the University of Chicago, and the Chicago Public School System), and the director of the program, Barbara Sizemore, a black sociologist trained at the Graduate School of Education of the University of Chicago. The university and the public school system were fully committed to the experiment, one of the first urban community school boards, and the board functioned well.

As was the case with many other involvements of the University of Chicago in the Woodlawn area, this project started with a completely different purpose. In the summer of 1965 a university-wide Committee on Urban Education began preparing plans to submit a proposal for an urban education laboratory. The proposal submitted in October 1965 was turned down because the Office of Education did not feel that there was enough community involvement. The Woodlawn Organization then exerted strong pressure to become a part of the project.

The mere working out of the ground rules prior to submission of a second proposal was complicated, and finally it was agreed that any one of the three parties represented on the proposed community school board could have a veto.

The Woodlawn Organization and the University of Chicago were both pleased with the proposal that was submitted in September

1966. They were shocked when late in November the Office of Education decided not to fund it. The university and TWO jointly sought to have the decision reconsidered and made forceful representations to the Secretary of Health, Education, and Welfare, John Gardner, and the Commissioner of Education, Harold Howe. In January 1967, the Office of Education reversed itself and awarded the funds.

Little remained of the University of Chicago's original unilateral idea for a research and development center in urban education. The Woodlawn Organization wanted basic changes made in the educational system and was not interested in "superficial or compensatory educational programs."

The original director of the program was Willard J. Congreve, a white professor at the University of Chicago's Graduate School of Education. He eventually resigned voluntarily because, although his staff was all black, he thought it was more appropriate that the program have black leadership as well.

In two of its early projects, the Woodlawn Experimental School Program tried to improve the teaching staff and to deal with gangs. Most of the teachers whom the board wanted to replace transferred voluntarily, and there was little confrontation with the teachers' union. Strong efforts were made to recruit outstanding teachers. A major attempt was made to eliminate warfare between the gangs because of the extent to which in these confrontations they intimidated students attempting to get to school.

In addition to making improvements in the schools, the Woodlawn Experimental School Program was instrumental in starting a community education center for adults, which operates at one of the schools and offers a wide range of programs from recreation to computer courses.

The University of Chicago not only was instrumental in securing the original funding but also served an important role in legitimating the project. Its involvement in Woodlawn was part of a whole new urban emphasis at the Graduate School of Education. Fringe benefits to the Woodlawn Experimental School Program have been other urban projects in which the School of Education has been involved.

From the experience of the Woodlawn Experimental School Program, Willard Congreve distinguished five separate functions in which the community and the educators interact. They are summarized in Table 1.

	Function	Person accountable	Person taking action
TABLE 1 **Community- educator interaction in school programs**	Goal setting	Client	Client with help from educator
	Program design	Educator	Educator with help from client
	Sanction and support	Client	Client with help from educator
	Program implementation	Educator	Educator with help from client
	Evaluation	Client	Client with help from educator

The Model Cities program for education was based specifically on the experiences of the Woodlawn Experimental School Program, but the plan called for adding new functions and increased coordination. The educational programs of public and parochial schools are to be coordinated, and educational services are to be expanded to include a preschool center, a career vocational institute, and a "fluid school" relying heavily on different kinds of educators, such as trained parents.

Economic Development A major feature of the Model Cities plan, and one in which the University of Chicago has not been much involved previously is the area of economic development. It is estimated that at least 10,000 persons in a potential Woodlawn work force of 35,000 need significant amounts of help. The idea of relying primarily on black entrepreneurs was discounted because they could not develop enough jobs. If there is substantial construction in the physical redevelopment of the Woodlawn area, this will provide a number of construction jobs. Many black people are already at work in the manpower training program and the rehabilitation of school facilities as part of the Woodlawn Experimental School Program. The Woodlawn Organization has participated in many federal and local employment programs by providing recruitment, selection, support, and education services. As a community organization with extensive block organization, it holds a comparative advantage in outreach and follow-up activities on the job front. The Model Cities plan calls for the education system to play a major role in preparing people for meaningful employment.

Arthur Brazier of The Woodlawn Organization is well aware that economic development and the securing of jobs are difficult areas that often involve conflict with the white power structure. In his opinion it was the white power structure within both the city of Chicago and the United States Senate that brought to a halt one of the most promising manpower training programs that The Wood-lawn Organization had started.

With funding from the Office of Economic Opportunity at the rate of approximately $1 million a year, The Woodlawn Organization started a program aimed at training gang members for meaningful employment. A prerequisite to securing the grant was The Woodlawn Organization's success in bringing about a truce between two gangs—the Blackstone Rangers and the Eastside Disciples. The city administration blocked appointment of the project director that The Woodlawn Organization wanted, and the police harassed the project throughout its year of existence. The press made sensational statements about the criminal involvement of some members of the project, and the U.S. Senate Subcommittee on Investigations held public hearings on the project and brought such pressure to bear on the Office of Economic Opportunity that the project was not refunded.

Although the university was not formally involved in either the drafting of the proposal or the operation of the program, it offered strong support to The Woodlawn Organization in an effort to keep the program going. Julian Levi attempted to get Mayor Daley to back the program. Irving Spergel of the School of Social Service administration evaluated the program and defended it strongly.

SUMMARY The university has become involved in a number of programs in the Woodlawn area, and each has been reshaped to meet the specific needs of the people of Woodlawn. Initial hostility between the University of Chicago and The Woodlawn Organization has been replaced by a working relationship in which TWO calls the shots and the university supplies the expertise and sometimes the resources. The university's rationale for becoming involved in these projects was not simply to provide services, but rather to learn about new methods of delivering services. The desire of The Woodlawn Organization to draw up a new Model Cities plan allowed the experiences of a number of separate units to be distilled into a comprehensive program that has wide applicability to other universities and cities.

This brief description of what transpired in Woodlawn does not intend to give the impression that all the hurdles have been passed and that everything in the future will be a success. However, anyone looking at the record cannot fail to be impressed by the large accomplishments. Key ingredients in this story have been pragmatic, forceful leadership both at the University of Chicago and in The Woodlawn Organization.

References

Beadle, Muriel: *The Hyde Park-Kenwood Urban Renewal Years: A History to Date,* University of Chicago, October 1964.

Brazier, Arthur M.: *Black Self-determination: The Story of The Woodlawn Organization,* Williams B. Berdmans Publishing Company, Grand Rapids, Mich., 1969.

Bruckner, D. J. R.: "Unique City Plan Formed in Chicago: Black Community's Leaders Will Seek Approval by Daley," *Los Angeles Times,* Nov. 29, 1968.

Congreve, Willard J.: "The Woodlawn Experiment: Unique Collaboration," *Compact,* p. 22, April 1969.

Gunther, John: "Chicago Revisited," *Chicago Today,* vol. 2, no. 1, 1965.

Levi, Julian H.: "The Greatest Domestic Challenge," *Chicago Today,* vol. 5, pp. 2–8, Summer 1968.

Levi, Julian H.: "The Influence of Environment on Urban Institutions," *Educational Record,* vol. 42, pp. 137–141, April 1961.

Levi, Julian H.: "The Neighborhood Program of the University of Chicago," paper prepared for the Office of Education, Department of Health, Education and Welfare, for inclusion in a casebook, August 1961.

Nash, George, and Particia Nash: "Leads Columbia Could Have Followed," *New York,* June 3, 1968. Reprint no. A-549, Bureau of Applied Social Research, Columbia University, New York.

Rossi, Peter H., and Robert A. Dentler: *The Politics of Urban Renewal: The Chicago Findings,* Free Press of Glencoe, New York, 1961.

Schiff, Sheldon K.: "Community Accountability and Mental Health Services," *Mental Hygiene,* vol. 54, pp. 205–214, April 1970.

Swenson, William: *The Continuing Colloquium on University of Chicago Demonstration Projects in Woodlawn: Aspects of a Major University's Commitment to an Inner-city Ghetto,* report prepared for the Department of Housing and Urban Development, University of Chicago, Center for Urban Studies, 1968.

U.S. Commission on Civil Rights: *T.W.O.'s Model Cities Plan,* Clearinghouse Publication, Urban Series no. 2, Washington, D.C., 1969.

Williams, Eddie N. (ed.): *Delivery Systems for Model Cities: New Concepts in Serving the Urban Community,* University of Chicago, Center for Policy Study and Center for Urban Studies, 1969.

3. Southern Illinois University: Growth Through Service

Friends and foes alike agree that Delyte Morris, the president of Southern Illinois University (SIU) and guiding hand in its meteoric growth from obscurity, is a dynamic leader. He recently asked to become president emeritus at the age of 62 and gave up active stewardship of SIU after 21 years. This chapter attempts to recount how Morris involved SIU in service to the once-impoverished southern Illinois region. His success in convincing citizens and state legislators that SIU had been of service has made the university's growth possible.

There is no question that SIU has provided service as an educator. When Morris arrived in the fall of 1948, there were 3,300 students on a one-square-block campus in Carbondale, 100 miles southeast of St. Louis, Missouri. In the academic year 1969–70, there were 23,000 students at SIU's Carbondale campus and another 12,000 at the Edwardsville campus 20 miles east of St. Louis. Graduate enrollment increased 20 times, from 250 students to 5,000. For years SIU had a virtually open admissions policy, and thus many of its students probably would not have gone to college elsewhere.

In the area surrounding Carbondale, the university achieved a great deal of success by pioneering in imaginative community building. Its Community Development Services unit once was an active developer of the small, impoverished towns that dot the region. Over the years it has become much more academic, and now it emphasizes instruction and research.

When Community Development Services attempted to revitalize an urban area with a sizable black population—East St. Louis, Illinois—it failed. The methods that had proved successful in the south did not apply, political factors interfered, and the problems of the city were more severe. Despite its unsuccessful efforts in East

St. Louis, SIU is now working to develop the metropolitan area east of St. Louis, Missouri, where its chances of success appear brighter.

The university has also been of service to the region as a major employer and purchaser of goods and services. Edwardsville and Carbondale are the two largest economic concentrations in southern Illinois. Their total revenues approach $100 million per year. President Morris stressed the bricks-and-mortar aspect of expansion, and the worth of the physical plant rose from $5 million in 1948 to a present value of $200 million with another $100 million in construction under way or being planned.

Although SIU may not be a powerhouse academically, it is fairly impressive. Over half of the 3,500 faculty members hold the doctorate, and they attract approximately $10 million in research grants each year. More than half a dozen interdisciplinary centers and institutes geared to broad concerns, such as labor and Latin American affairs, have been created on a permanent basis.

Southern Illinois University has attempted to serve three quite different sections of the region:

1 Extreme southern Illinois is the area between the Mississippi and the Ohio Rivers. It has no sizable cities. Since the coal mines gave out in the 1930s, the region has been economically depressed. The economic condition of some towns has improved in recent years, in part from the work of SIU's Community Development Services.

2 East St. Louis, Illinois, has long been the poor cousin across the river from St. Louis, Missouri. It is heavily industrial. In recent years it has become increasingly black in population (going from two-fifths in 1960 to approximately two-thirds in 1970). The population has declined from 85,000 to approximately 70,000. It is regarded as a troubled city.

3 The metropolitan area east of St. Louis is now referred to as Metro East. This region contains the only sizable cities in the southern half of Illinois. In addition to East St. Louis, there are Belleville, Granite City, and Alton. Edwardsville lies roughly in the center of this region. The area was generally underdeveloped, but it is now readily accessible to St. Louis, Missouri, because of recent interstate highway construction.

COMMUNITY DEVELOPMENT IN SOUTHERN ILLINOIS At the time Delyte Morris took over the presidency of SIU in the fall of 1948, an organization of businessmen, Southern Illinois, Inc., was already interested in promoting education in and general development of the region.

Morris learned of Baker Brownell, a philosopher primarily interested in the small community as a basis of democratic life. Brownell was soon to retire from Northwestern University. He agreed to come to the SIU campus, and under his leadership the Area Services Plan of Southern Illinois University was developed.

At the suggestion of Brownell, the university hired Richard Poston to assume the leadership of the newly created Community Development Services. With his arrival in 1953, the university became a major force in the renewal of communities in southern Illinois.

As Poston saw it, one of the principal deficits of southern Illinois was a feeling of hopelessness on the part of its residents. There were two competing groups of miners and a history of bitter labor-management strife. A national factory-locating service had just dealt the region a major blow by recommending against locating new factories there because of labor unrest.

Poston wanted to start his program in southern Illinois with a quick, visible success in one town, which would give him access to others. Even before he arrived from Washington, publicity was disseminated about what SIU was hoping to do in community development. A labor group in Eldorado, Illinois, a small town of 4,000 people, asked the university for help in September 1953.

Poston's first response was to get the community to make an investment and to begin to work together. The organization that had contacted the university was asked to assemble a representative group of town residents for a meeting at the university to discuss what might be done. Poston told them that the two rival newspapers would have to work together and that labor and management would have to bury their differences and cooperate. The project was to be a self-help effort, with the university providing leadership and staff but not funds. Citizen response was enthusiastic from the start.

Drama and public relations were used to involve the citizenry in community self-analysis and local problem solving. The first step was a gala outdoor rally in October, attended by a number of politicians and university officials. Poston was the principal speaker. He stood in his shirtsleeves and gave an inspiring 45-minute talk painting the future that could be realized if only the people would work together.

Not surprisingly, the first step was a study. However, the primary purpose of the research was to get people involved in planning the future of their town. The data for the study were to come from a census of all town residents. Since the purpose was to get as many citizens involved as possible, 300 people were enrolled as census takers. The week of training they received was their first experience in community development and working together.

The census was kicked off with a bang: a pancake breakfast for the census takers. Handbills had already been distributed to all households announcing the census, and it had been described at length in the newspapers. Church bells and fire sirens heralded its beginning.

Two weeks later, 1,000 people gathered to discuss the preliminary results of the census. They broke up into 15 working committees to study specific issues, such as beautification, the library, and industrial development. Group discussion leaders and note takers each received special training. Town meetings were held over the next few months to hear recommendations from the study groups. These were mass meetings with as many as 2,000 people attending.

This was research with a different twist. Instead of being done by the experts as an alternative to action, it was done by the citizens as a first step in finding possible solutions to their problems. Correct methodology, exact findings, and journal publication were not the goals. Rather the aim was to let the people determine what their problems were, so that they could begin to formulate their own solutions.

One of the first and most popular activities undertaken by Community Development Services in Eldorado was beautification. The city hall was remodeled with volunteer labor. Then, once people learned how to do it and saw that their neighbors were doing it, they began to spruce up their neighborhoods and their houses.

From the outset it was clear that a prime community goal was to attract industry and improve the economic condition of the town. Community Development Services helped organize six small local industries and brought two manufacturing operations to town. Poston worked personally with each of the manufacturers to help solve their problems.

By the spring of 1954 Eldorado was the visible success that Poston had hoped for. Area newspapers gave the town's story a great deal of attention. Eldorado won the top civic award of the American Freedoms Foundation and was named an "all-American city" by *Look* magazine. Edward R. Murrow featured Eldorado in a one-hour *See It Now* television documentary. The residents had planned to convert a four-acre run-down area into a park. To make the television show more dramatic and to show what a community could do when it set its mind to it, the park was built in one day. Starting at dawn, 385 truckloads of dirt were brought in and bulldozed into place. By the time dusk fell, the park was being seeded.

Success in Eldorado led to a host of requests from other communities, and Community Development Services began a large-scale operation that continued for the next six years. By 1960 full programs had been conducted in more than 20 communities. The budget of Community Development Services went from $24,000 per year to $250,000, and by 1960 a staff of 17 was at work.

Poston realized that economic development was essential for community development. An industrial development specialist, Robert Henderson, was appointed to the staff despite the fact that he had not attended college. He and Poston secured funds from local utility companies to use for entertaining visiting industrialists and to pay for exhibit space at industrial fairs. They worked with Chicago bankers to make credit available in southern Illinois, and they persuaded industrial rating firms to recommend southern Illinois as an industrial site. In six years industries with annual payrolls in excess of $60 million moved into the area. Community Development Services also helped start locally owned industries, such as a tomato growers' cooperative.

In his years in southern Illinois, Poston developed and promulgated a philosophy that is best summarized by the title of his book, *Democracy Is You* (1953). The primary need was to help the citizens organize themselves to build a community that would encompass all civic interest groups but would rise above individual interests. Poston's statements were evangelistic and optimistic, but they recognized that professionals and technicians can make a larger contribution to community renewal when the citizens themselves assume responsibility and direction.

To aid the communities being renewed, Poston and his staff developed how-to-do-it manuals with sections on beautification, recreation, housing, culture, and social welfare and with lists of regional and national resources. Typical of the information offered was that on housing. The manual suggested that neighbors swap time with each other to perform difficult tasks, that local merchants be urged to sponsor housing clinics, that neighborhood improvement contests be carried out, and that paint-up, clean-up, and similar campaigns be mounted. The manual also offered advice on zoning, building regulations, and home improvement loans, and it listed the public officials responsible for maintaining housing standards.

The idea was always to organize as many groups as possible into a cooperative effort and to involve as many citizens as possible. In the larger towns, people were organized on a neighborhood basis. An account written by one of Poston's staff members about the organization of one urban neighborhood is a case in point. A woman called city hall to complain that a junkyard was being planned for the vacant lot next to her house. She had intended merely to register a complaint.

She was referred to a consultant from Community Development Services, who told her that if she would arrange a meeting of neighbors to discuss the matter, he would join them. By the following evening she had gathered together a group of neighbors, most of whom had never done anything together before. The consultant used their concern about the junkyard as a means of getting the community to organize itself. It took a number of meetings and a lot of effort, but eventually a viable community organization was formed, which accomplished much more than just keeping the junkyard out.

At the same time that Community Development Services was achieving success in renewing towns and cities in southern Illinois, it was being transformed by academic pressures. New personnel with Ph.D.'s were being hired by CDS as a result of university demands.

Academic background was not a problem to Richard Poston. He had not pursued the standard graduate training nor had he climbed the traditional academic ladder from assistant to full professor with progress rewarded because of publications. He was a sociologist interested in effecting change. To reward his success, Delyte Morris promoted Poston to a full research professorship in 1960. Research professorships at SIU are academic rewards conferring on their holders virtually no fixed responsibilities but rather the ability to do what they see fit. Since 1960, Poston has studied and engaged in community development and urban sociology in many parts of the world, but he has had little contact with Community Development Services and southern Illinois.

Under different and more traditionally academic leadership, Community Development Services has shifted to a heavier emphasis on instruction. The research is now more traditional, and most of it is done by experts. CDS has become outstanding in both research and instruction, but the beneficiaries have been primarily the students, many of whom are former Peace Corps volunteers, and the faculty. The number of students enrolled in its program has increased from just 2 in 1966 to 66 in 1970. Comprehensive community-wide development is no longer emphasized.

The present director, Richard Thomas, feels that many of the former functions of Community Development Services have been taken over by various federal government programs. To help communities, the SIU unit now stresses research. It is developing a program of aerial photography to record benchmark data on the state of the region. Present projects are primarily individual efforts that will aid both individual communities and the region but will not revitalize communities.

In 1968, a very different sort of service was started within Community Development Services at Carbondale. Because it was a new and unique approach, it caused some internal conflict and was later separated from that unit. The vice-president of the Area and International Services, Ralph W. Ruffner, brought in Walter Robinson to head University Services to Carbondale. Robinson, a black, had previously served as director of the Neighborhood Youth Corps in East St. Louis. He defined the task of his new office as determining how the university could best serve the disadvantaged persons and communities of southern Illinois, giving priority to black communities. The emphasis was not on teaching or research.

Robinson was active in helping the black university students in Carbondale to organize the Black American Studies program. He helped them start a newspaper, which also served the black community of Carbondale. In Cairo, Illinois, he worked with blacks to organize a cooperative supermarket. His office acted as a broker matching the needs of the black community for specific types of education, technical assistance, and recreation with the resources and competencies of the university.

Despite the fact that SIU at Carbondale has the second largest population of black students of all major universities (the first is at Wayne State), there are relatively few blacks on the faculty, and black students felt that they had a host of problems both on and off the campus. Now the Carbondale campus has the beginnings of a good black studies program, an impressive black students' center, and a program to recruit and train black faculty. The university is serving as an example in the area of black and white relations for the region in which it is located.

Southern Illinois University has served another important educational need in southern Illinois. In 1953 it opened the Vocational and Technical Institute, which provides the equivalent of a technical junior college curriculum, leading to an associate's degree, and gives adult noncredit extension courses. The institute is the largest school of its type in southern Illinois, with 1,500 students enrolled in 28 fields. It offers a wide range of technical courses, such as architectural, automotive, and aviation technology, mortuary science, and commercial art. The Vocational and Technical Institute has also operated programs for poor blacks in East St. Louis and programs in prisons.

In combination, SIU at Carbondale and the Vocational and Technical Institute located 10 miles away offer a broad range of education at low cost to an area that once was virtually bereft of institutions of higher education. One reason that each was able to expand so rapidly was that almost any high school graduate could attend. This has led to an increased demand for education, so that each of the institutions is now forced to be more selective. However, both SIU and the institute allow students who rank low in their high school graduating classes to enroll in the spring semester, while restricting enrollment for the fall semester to those who rank higher.

One reason that SIU was able to proceed so imaginatively in the area of community development in southern Illinois was Delyte Morris's willingness to innovate. In hiring Richard Poston and his early associates in Community Development Services, Morris considered the ability to produce more important than academic credentials. Innovation can also produce failure or controversy, however, and SIU experienced this as well. Its operation of a Job Corps Center in Breckenridge, Kentucky, was not regarded as successful, and the camp was switched to the control of a private corporation. University officials engaged in the Job Corps Center project feel that they learned something from the program, even though the university itself suffered.

UNIVERSITY INVOLVEMENT IN EAST ST. LOUIS

Southern Illinois University's record in East St. Louis has been far less successful than that of Community Development Services in the southern region of Illinois. With the aid of consultants from Community Development Services, a citywide organization named Community Progress Incorporated was started in East St. Louis in 1957. It had a 21-member board of directors, representing most community organizations. Fact-finding committees were established in areas such as education, recreation, and government. Attempts were made to organize local neighborhoods and to bring the leaders of these neighborhood organizations together. Progress was slow and the results disappointing.

The first town meeting was not held until November 1959, and it and other community-wide meetings were not regarded as successful. Lack of success was attributed partly to racial tensions and partly to the fact that local issues were considered more important than community-wide issues. For a variety of reasons, no strong organization having widespread community support emerged. This meant that subsequent programs undertaken by the university and the federal government in East St. Louis were individual, unrelated efforts that did not build upon one another.

There were two further reasons why the efforts to form a strong community in East St. Louis failed:

1   Because of the complexity of problems in East St. Louis, the job was more difficult than the university originally envisioned. Community Development Services operated a vigorous program for three years—the period that Richard Poston had predicted would be necessary. However, much more help was still needed. When Poston left in 1960 and the mission of Community Development Services changed, the program became less aggressive and more academic. Lila Teer, who participated in the initial efforts to organize East St. Louis in 1957 and is now SIU's coordinator of programs in East St. Louis, believes that progress was being made and that if the same vigor had been pursued for the next several years there would have been much more to show for the entire effort.

2   The white power structure pinned many of its hopes on the presence of SIU in East St. Louis. When the Edwardsville campus opened in 1965 and most units of SIU that had been located in East St. Louis were pulled out, some members of the white power structure left the city. Had SIU built its campus in East St. Louis, the story might have ended very differently; but East St. Louis did not have room for the massive type of campus that SIU wanted.

Gene Graves, an assistant to President Morris and former director of business and economic development for the state of Illinois, was one of the original Community Development Services consultants in East St. Louis. He feels that the university failed there because it did not become involved with political problems in a partisan sense. In his opinion the university had many opportunities for direct action that it did not take. For example, it did a study that showed how bad the housing situation was, but then failed to take the next step and get involved in the building of housing. Graves feels there is a real anti-SIU backlash in East St. Louis now. "The University should have avoided inflicting on the community associate professors with all the answers. SIU has been a crutch in East St. Louis. It should have been a catalyst."

Despite the fact the Southern Illinois University was unable to bring about the birth of an enduring community organization, many people who were active in Community Progress Incorporated are now involved in the East St. Louis Model Cities program. A large proportion of the Model Cities leadership got its first taste of action in the early community work of SIU.

The Edwardsville campus has never become involved in community development the way Carbondale did. It has a Regional and Urban Development unit, but its major aims are providing data and doing evaluations. Much of its research has focused on East St. Louis. Staff from the unit were loaned to the city to assist in developing a Model Cities proposal, and the unit has continued to assist the Model Cities program.

In its last years in East St. Louis, SIU began a number of special educational programs which may raise the productivity of the area and help to generate new black leadership.

Katherine Dunham, the distinguished black dancer, set up the Performing Arts Training Center and Dynamic Museum, which has been quite successful. It trains teachers in the performing arts, serves as a recreation and training center for young black children, and is a museum and library of black art and culture. It is funded in part by the Office of Economic Opportunity and the Danforth and Rockefeller Foundations, and, although it is not specifically connected with the university, university assistance is available to it.

The university established the Experiment in Higher Education, funded by the Office of Economic Opportunity, for 200 students. It was one of the first challenging open-enrollment college programs for black urban students with poor academic backgrounds. The Experiment accepted all high school graduates; most of its students were poorly prepared for college. Based on the performance of its students there and at the colleges to which they transferred for their last two years, the Experiment was a success. The backbone of the program was a dedicated faculty recruited from around the country on the basis of the members' willingness to teach, work hard, and relate to ghetto students rather than on the basis of their credentials. Many had only B.A.'s.

The program had tremendous symbolic effect on colleges throughout the country, as it demonstrated that poorly prepared students could be "turned on" and enabled to succeed academically. Its philosophy was antiremedial. "Remedial programs lower kids' aspirations," says Ed Crosby, the black, bearded former associate director of the program (who has a doctorate in German). "We want to challenge students and to raise their aspirations. If a student has trouble with reading we give him *Candy* (the racy best seller) and a dictionary, not a remedial text. A black student who has survived 20 years in the ghetto has a tremendous amount of savvy and ability; otherwise he'd be dead. He has to learn new ways of doing things and new values. We try to make our students realize that education is a good hustle."

The program was successful because SIU was willing to experiment with really new forms and philosophies and to ignore the lack of credentials. However, like much radical innovation, it did not endure at the level on which it began. The original faculty members were recruited away to start similar programs at other institutions. The program's distance from the Edwardsville campus, the establishment of a new community college, and SIU's withdrawal from East St. Louis all worked against it. The Experiment demonstrated SIU's willingness and ability to innovate, but at present its future is problematic.

The real impact of the Experiment in Higher Education was on other colleges and universities, which have started similar programs. From the start, the Experiment wanted to prove that such a program would succeed; it developed materials and techniques and it trained staff. Former staff members are now located at approximately 20 other institutions of higher education that have started similar programs. Principles developed by the Experiment have been incorporated into the new program of Special Services for the Disadvantaged of the U.S. Office of Education.

Southern Illinois University operates other service programs in East St. Louis. It is involved in a number of manpower development programs, and it offers technical assistance to various black enterprises. It continues to do research and evaluation, but many believe that East St. Louis has been researched to death.

A new community college that is independent of the university has been opened in East St. Louis. Although SIU wanted to operate the junior college, state officials decided against this. The fact that the community college is not related to the university has further weakened SIU's ability to serve the East St. Louis community.

Relations between SIU and the new college have not been cordial or cooperative.

The community college has been very aggressive in recruiting local black students. Free enrollment forms were printed in the local newspapers and 60 percent of the first students used these forms for their initial registration. Where SIU's Experiment in Higher Education enrolled 200 freshmen a year, the new community college has an enrollment of 1,000. The curriculum has been set up to facilitate transfer to the Edwardsville campus at the end of two years.

Until the fall of 1969, when the new community college opened, SIU operations were concentrated in several school buildings. At that time, the university returned the buildings to the local school system, which claimed to need them. One former SIU faculty member claims that conservative elements in East St. Louis pressed to get the buildings back as part of a move opposing SIU's efforts to improve the city. The few remaining SIU operations in East St. Louis are now less effective because they are dispersed throughout the city.

DEVELOPMENT IN METRO EAST Ever since the university established its campus at Edwardsville, it has worked to develop the metropolitan area east of St. Louis and in Illinois. Delyte Morris is chairman of the board of the Regional and Industrial Development Corporation, a six-county effort in both Missouri and Illinois.

It is still too early to tell how much success the university will have in developing Metro East. However, the giant new campus at Edwardsville has already made a major economic contribution to the region and should serve as a focal point for further development. Another organization with which SIU is involved—called Metro East—fights for the Illinois share of new facilities in the metropolitan area. For example, at present it is studying the feasibility of opening a second jet airport to serve the region. It would be located in Illinois.

In a major effort to make the region better known and to bring people from St. Louis, Missouri, across the river, Southern Illinois University has staged a Mississippi River festival on the Edwardsville campus. The festival has featured the St. Louis Symphony Orchestra and name performers such as Joan Baez and Van Cliburn. The festival can accommodate audiences of up to 15,000. It was first staged in the summer of 1969. That season it lost

$150,000 (partially in one-time setting-up costs), and it came in for considerable criticism. However, Delyte Morris is a tenacious person; when he thinks he has a good idea, he sees it through. It is probable that both the Mississippi River festival and Metro East regional development will be enduring successes.

The involvement and success of SIU in community development have largely been the result of Delyte Morris's willingness to pick good people without regard to academic qualifications and to give them freedom and resources. Not all the ventures have succeeded, and the greatest successes did not endure. This experience suggests that the role of the university in noneducational endeavors is to pioneer new forms and not to operate such programs on a permanent basis. More effort should be put into the dissemination of successful innovations.

Morris was successful because he kept in touch with the times and had long-range vision. At the same time he has been accused by some critics of being insensitive and ruthless. Two innovations — the University Services to Carbondale program and the black studies program — resulted when a group of black students occupied Morris's office. However, the students who led the effort were expelled and despite the fact that progress was made a bad taste was left in the mouths of some black students and faculty.

4. University of California, Los Angeles: Progress Despite Travail

Its country club setting in the Los Angeles suburb of Westwood makes the University of California, Los Angeles, seem unlikely to be deeply involved in urban, minority-group, and community affairs. But as an educator of a diversity of ethnic groups, UCLA has been a pioneer. Its involvement has been more centrally administered, received more support from the top, and followed a straighter line of progression than that of most colleges and universities. Despite high-level administrative commitment, UCLA's programs have run into a series of roadblocks and barriers that would have unsettled any college administration and caused the more faint-hearted to abandon their plans. The UCLA administration has, however, weathered a number of early storms, changed the specifics of most of their programs without abandoning their original goals, and developed several sound programs that should be long-lived.

This chapter will concentrate on just two of the many elements of UCLA's urban involvement: the ethnic centers program and its antecedents, the special education programs. These two are fairly unusual, and each had to be changed considerably during the early, troublesome, developmental phases.

Special education programs, beginning with the Educational Opportunity Program (EOP), started bringing in minority-group students, most of whom were black. The original students pushed for expansion of these programs and played a leading role in formulating the idea of four ethnic centers: Afro-American (black), Chicano (Mexican-American), American Indian (Native American), and Asian-American. All are now operating. UCLA is offering a whole series of programs aimed at these four ethnic groups.

THE CHANCELLOR'S TASK FORCES In May 1968, the new president of the University of California, Charles Hitch, presented a special report to the regents of the university entitled "What We Must Do: The University and

43

the Urban Crisis." He cited the need for "a concerted effort by the University to become viably involved in the present urban crisis."

Chancellor Charles Young of UCLA responded by appointing a steering committee to study the matter during the summer of 1968 and propose solutions. The steering committee was chaired by C. Z. Wilson, an extremely capable black assistant to Chancellor Young. Wilson assumed a leadership position in coordinating UCLA's attack on urban problems at that point, and this has continued as his major area of responsibility. He is now the vice-chancellor for academic programs, and his role is to be a planner and catalyst rather than to have administrative responsibility for operation of the programs.

The steering committee divided itself into three task forces, each under student chairmanship. Membership of the task forces extended beyond that of the steering committee and represented all segments of the campus community, with heavy student participation. The groups studied student entry, curriculum development, and urban research and action. By the end of the summer each had prepared detailed proposals for action.

The majority of the proposals that the steering committee made were adopted, and they have provided the framework for what was done subsequently. One reason the task forces were able to contribute so much was that UCLA had already made a substantial beginning at involvement in urban, community, and minority-group problems. The task force on student entry acknowledged the progress of existing opportunity programs for minority-group students at the undergraduate and graduate levels, and it proposed a series of new programs, the most important of which was the High Potential program (Hi-Pot). The constructiveness and creativity of the students involved in the task forces were most impressive, although many were thinking about important policy decisions for the first time in their lives.

THE SPECIAL EDUCATION PROGRAMS The variety of new special education programs at UCLA, added to those in existence prior to formation of the chancellor's task forces, had increased UCLA's undergraduate minority-group enrollment to 19 percent by the fall of 1969. Graduate minority enrollment reached 14 percent. Total graduate and undergraduate enrollment of black students by the fall of 1969 was 1,280. There were 940 Mexican-Americans and 180 American Indians. These were all among the highest totals for an institution of higher education in the United States as of that date. The largest minority group at UCLA, however, totaling 2,300 students or 8 percent of total enrollment, was the Oriental-Americans.

The Educational Opportunities Program (EOP)
The EOP program at UCLA was established in 1964 by Chancellor Franklin Murphy. Its 33 students were the first in a program that, by the academic year 1969–70, had spread to the entire California system of higher education, enrolling 5,300 students (4,200 undergraduates) at University of California campuses and another 3,150 students at the state colleges. The community college EOP program began operation in the academic year 1970–71. According to UCLA, its EOP program was the first major program in the United States assisting students of Mexican-American descent. By the academic year 1969–70, the largest EOP program was UCLA's, with 1,500 students.

There have been two evaluations of the EOP program: one by Weiler and Rogers on the UCLA program and one by Kitano and Miller on the entire EOP program at all California campuses. Each concluded that EOP students had done as well as or better than regularly admitted California freshmen. Each, however, was critical of the EOP program for taking only the best minority-group students.

To understand the functioning of the EOP program, one has to consider the California statewide plan for higher education, to which all the individual campuses in the system must adhere. It has come under considerable attack. The system is stratified: the nine branches of the University of California get most of the students with highest academic grades, the state college system gets the next best, and the community colleges get the residue. The three types of institutions vary not only in the quality of their student bodies, but also in per capita allocation, proportion of students living on campus, quality of faculty, and drop-out rate. Every high school graduate is assured the opportunity to pursue postsecondary education, but the opportunities presented to those who do better in high school are much greater. To introduce some flexibility into the system, the universities were allowed to accept, as up to 2 percent of the entering freshmen class and transfer students, applicants who would not ordinarily qualify for admission to the university system. (Ordinarily only students ranking in the top 12½ percent of their high school graduating class are eligible for the university system.) When universities throughout the country began trying to reduce the underrepresentation of minority-group students, this figure was increased to 4 percent, with at least 2 percent always reserved for undergraduate EOP and other special education programs. This means that UCLA, with 13,500 undergraduates and 4,877 freshmen and transfer students, could accept up to 200 students who did not meet the normal standards for admission. When UCLA began the EOP program, it found that a large number of capable minority-group students could be expected to do well at the university, although they had not performed quite well enough in high school or on admissions tests.

Of those enrolled in the fall of 1968, 31 percent were black and 25 percent had Spanish surnames. An analysis of the qualifications of the EOP students showed that many were actually eligible for admission to UCLA, but that most probably would not have gone. Why, then, hadn't they simply applied for UCLA in the regular fashion? The evaluators concluded that there were three reasons: finances, geography, and culture.

The EOP program sought to deal with each of these problems:

1 *Geography* Most minority-group students live far from the UCLA campus, and public transportation is notoriously bad in the Los Angeles area. To overcome this, the EOP program sent recruiters to predominantly minority-group high schools whose students had never considered the possibility of UCLA, and funds were provided for EOP students to live on campus.

2 *Finances* The EOP students were given whatever financial aid they needed to enroll at UCLA. State funds were combined with grants from the Rockefeller and Danforth Foundations, and the largest sources of funds were three federal financial aid programs: Educational Opportunity Grants, National Defense Student Loans, and College Work-Study program jobs. For the academic year 1969–70, the aid funds available to the 1,500 EOP students at UCLA totaled approximately $1,900,000 or about $1,300 per student. It was estimated that a student's total cost of attending college (and living on campus) was approximately $2,000. Each student's financial situation was assessed individually, and no student was denied access to the program on financial grounds.

3 *Culture* One of the reasons minority-group students had not been attending UCLA was that they had grown up and gone to high school in predominantly minority-group settings. The university, as a predominantly white institution, represented a different way of life and, for many of these students, a real culture shock. The UCLA staff attempted to ameliorate this

by counseling and tutoring. Each EOP student was assigned a master tutor, usually a graduate student, who served as a big brother and helped to explain the functioning of the academic system. Each student was also counseled fairly extensively by the EOP staff, the majority of whom were minority-group members. The counseling and tutoring were expensive: UCLA spent about $520,000 or $350 per student on this phase of the program in the academic year 1969–70. (The campus's proportion of the total university system expenditure of nearly $8 million was approximately one-third.)

The EOP assembled minority-group students in sufficient numbers so that they were able to make demands on the university that led to many of UCLA's subsequent programs. A large proportion of the students on the chancellor's task forces had been admitted under EOP. It was because of EOP that the black and Chicano student organizations became impcrtant forces on campus.

The High Potential Program (Hi-Pot) The principal contribution of the student entry task force of the chancellor's steering committee was the Hi-Pot program, which was begun in the fall quarter of the academic year 1968–69. The aim was to enroll minority-group members who had the potential to absorb higher education but were clearly inadmissible by present university standards. The recruiters for the program were black and Chicano students already enrolled at UCLA, who were paid for six weeks' work.

Approximately 400 students were located and interviewed, and the student recruiters recommended 60 blacks and 60 Chicanos for admission to the university. The 120 students were then screened by a faculty committee that finally recommended 50 blacks and 48 Chicanos. The average age of the group was 21. The population was two-thirds male and one-third female. One-third of the blacks and one-fifth of the Chicanos had previously been enrolled in junior college.

The stated criteria for recognizing high potential in applicants were basic intelligence, self-assurance, motivation, and endurance.

The staff members of the Hi-Pot program were selected on the basis of their empathy for the goals of the program. There were two administrators and eight instructors—four blacks and four Chicanos. Five of the instructors were graduate students at the university. The entire staff was interviewed and approved by members of UCLA's English and history departments.

The Hi-Pot program was conceived as a five-year program. The first year was to be spent primarily in preparatory and remedial education, with students first being instructed entirely by the High Potential staff and gradually moving into the regular curriculum.

The budget for the first year of the program was approximately $225,000. Most of the money came from student registration fees. Administratively, the program was joined with the Upward Bound program, already in existence at UCLA, and the Educational Opportunities Program to form the Department of Special Educational Programs under the direction of Mary Jane Hewitt.

The curriculum of the Hi-Pot program was organized around two basic objectives:

1 To give the student a positive self-concept by providing opportunities for exploration, analysis, and understanding of the Afro-American and Chicano experience in American society

2 To develop basic communication skills (oral and written) and reading skills (speed and comprehension) that are needed for success at the university

The educational programs for black and Chicano students were separate. In each, the emphasis at first was on developing a positive self-concept, and only later was also placed on developing communication skills. In the first quarter, black students had four courses: "The Negro Dialect," "The Afro-American Oral Tradition," "The Changing Status of the Black Man in White America," and "The Afro-American Literary Experience." In the second quarter, the initiative changed to an emphasis on communication skills, and the black students had one regular university course which was specially geared for them — "Recurring Philosophical Themes in Black Literature."

By the third quarter, 80 percent of the students were enrolled in at least some standard university courses. The statistical results of the first year's program were fairly encouraging considering the fact that the students were recruited late in the summer and would not have been considered eligible for admission to the university.

The High Potential program encountered serious problems at first. There was high turnover among the instructional staff, in part because the first staff had been recruited at the last minute. There were complaints that the students had been picked for political reasons — that is, their involvement in ethnic power movements — rather than for their potential as students in college. There were complaints from the Department of Special Educational Programs that the High Potential staff did not coordinate sufficiently with other elements in the program. This led to turnover and dissatisfaction within the unit that was supposed to coordinate all special education programs. In the summer of 1970 the High Potential program was reorganized to deal with problems of admission and of coordination with the other special programs.

Special Programs for High School Students

The Summer Work Opportunity program gave Los Angeles high school students the opportunity to work on a variety of research projects at UCLA during the summer. ·

The College Commitment program allowed UCLA undergraduates (principally blacks) to work in high schools to help minority-group students learn about and plan to attend college. This program also engaged in tutoring. One of its high points was a Career Day held at a high school, where black people spoke to the students about their occupations and how to prepare for them. The program basically depended on student volunteer work, and there have been problems in administration and in getting enough students to do the work.

Graduate-level Educational Opportunity Programs

There has been an extensive effort to increase the number of minority-group students at the master's and doctoral levels. The UCLA Law School sponsored a joint summer program with Loyola University to prepare minority-group students for law school. The Graduate Schools of Education and Business have each offered a variety of scholarships to minority-group students. All these programs helped to raise the minority-group graduate enrollment at UCLA to 14 percent by the academic year 1969–70.

The faculty development program has aimed to bring to the university 20 to 30 professionals a year on academic appointments in various fields and to provide support so that they could obtain doctorates while teaching a limited course load. The university has also changed its policy against hiring its own graduates, because it now feels that the best way to increase minority-group representation on the faculty is to train its own minority-group faculty.

The Upward Bound Program

At UCLA there is a fairly substantial Upward Bound program (an Office of Education college preparatory program) under the direction of the Department of Special Educational Programs. Students in Upward Bound at UCLA have been a major presence at the university. Their presence in Campbell Hall helps to establish it as the center for ethnic minorities on campus. Special efforts have been made to assure that graduates of Upward Bound are enrolled in UCLA as undergraduates.

Programs Proposed but Not Undertaken

The chancellor's task forces proposed two additional programs to help ethnic minorities that were not implemented. The Bombed-Out program was conceived as a way to give a second chance to students who had flunked out of the University of California system.

The junior college liaison program would have brought the institutions in the University of California system into close working relationships with the junior colleges in their areas to encourage a higher proportion of minority-group students to transfer to the university system after completing their first two years at community colleges.

The Veterans Special Education Program

The Extension Division of UCLA has begun a special program to educate minority-group veterans and to prepare them to attend college. It offers a 12-week course, charging the minimal sum of $100, and the veterans are eligible to obtain GI benefits of $175 per month while enrolled. Because there is a lag between applying to the Veterans Administration and receiving funds, the program has made $250 loans available to those who needed them, and it has provided scholarships to those who could not afford the $100 fee. The course is conducted in downtown Los Angeles, rather than at the more inaccessible UCLA campus. The extension program has been quite successful: approximately 80 percent of those completing it enroll in college, many at UCLA.

FROM SPECIAL EDUCATION PROGRAMS TO ETHNIC CENTERS

A large proportion of colleges and universities now offer special education programs for students who would not normally be admissible; UCLA differs from the vast majority in the range of programs offered and in the number of students enrolled. The large number of minority-group students who came in through these programs made the ethnic centers a possibility. Two factors are especially impressive at UCLA: the extensive role the students played in planning the programs, and the speed with which the university implemented large-scale programs. The ethnic centers are the subject of the balance of this chapter.

Planning of the Centers

The ethnic centers program, which grew out of the chancellor's task forces in the summer of 1968, was marked by controversy, ambiguity, conflict, and discord from the beginning. All four centers — Afro-American, Chicano, American Indian, and Asian-American — were operating by the fall of 1970, but only the Afro-American and American Indian centers had full-time directors by that time. All had immense problems in the first two years, including turnover of administrative personnel, changes in goals and orientation, lack of cooperation and coordination with each other, and strife with the administration over function, funds, staffing, and space. However, despite all the problems, Chancellor Young and Vice-Chancellor Wilson were committed to the concept of the four ethnic centers, and these are now emerging as viable entities directed by the ethnic groups themselves.

The idea for the centers came from the black students who were involved on the chancellor's task forces in the summer of 1968. They originally prepared a document entitled "Social Relevancy and the University," which was an inventory of what was already being done at the University, and they suggested the creation of a Center for the Study of Afro-American History and Culture. The work of the center would have been mostly research.

During the academic year 1968–69, the ethnic centers program was under the administrative responsibility of Paul Proehl, the vice-chancellor for university relations and public programs. He approved the concept, but he had a very specific idea about how the four ethnic centers would function in an Institute for American Cultures. His idea was based on his experience as director of UCLA's African Studies Center, a research unit which had been turning out quality scholarly materials on such subjects as the African arts. Proehl's idea was that the centers would be fairly traditional academic research units staffed by "fully qualified professionals." This was almost totally at variance with what the students envisioned and what had come into existence by the fall of 1970.

Each of the four centers has evolved a special character. There was heavy student involvement in each, and each has sought to aid the education at UCLA of its particular minority group. The thrust of both the Afro-American Center and the Chicano Cultural Center is to uplift the self-image of blacks and Chicanos. All four centers have been involved in service to their communities.

Physical Facilities The ethnic centers and the special education programs are located in Campbell Hall. Originally the building had been promised to the English and Slavic languages departments, and money had been set aside to remodel it for their use. The ethnic programs were placed there only temporarily. But, with all the travail that the programs underwent, Campbell Hall took on a special significance. In the fall of 1969, Chancellor Young decided that the ethnic centers and the special education programs could be permanently housed there.

The condition of the building itself in the summer of 1970 told a lot about the problems the programs had experienced. The building was crowded and bustling, with few white faces in evidence. However, the contrast between the attractive, well-landscaped UCLA campus and the decrepit interior of Campbell Hall would be something of a shock to a first-time visitor. Because the centers are still in transition and no overall plan for remodeling the building has been settled on, the interior is dirty and run-down, with the walls covered by graffiti. The individual offices are in considerably better shape than the public spaces, but the furnishings are still far from permanent, and there is a great deal of casualness and disorder.

The Afro-American Studies Center

In January 1969, Chancellor Young announced that the four ethnic study centers would begin operations and that their emphasis would be on research. Since the beginning of the ethnic centers program, the Afro-American Studies Center has been the most controversial.

The murder of two Black Panther High Potential students in Campbell Hall on January 19 was a shocking and tragic event that made national news. It was the outgrowth of a power struggle between Los Angeles black leader (and former UCLA student) Ron Karenga, the leader of an organization entitled US, and the local Black Panther group. A number of black leaders in the Los Angeles area had banded together to make sure that blacks would have a say in programs affecting them. They had proposed that Charles Thomas, a psychologist and education director of the Watts Health Center, be named the director of the Afro-American Studies Center. Originally, students in the Black Students Union had felt that it was important to express solidarity, and they had worked with the Los Angeles black community leaders in urging the administration to appoint Thomas. The administration objected, however, primarily on the ground that the clinical psychologist was not entitled either to a $23,000 salary or to tenure, and they offered him $16,000. Some black students began to have doubts about Thomas's commitment to their program; they felt, with resentment, that he was being pushed on them by outsiders, and they wanted to withdraw their support.

A black student who had participated in plans for the Afro-American Studies Center from the beginning noted that in the weeks prior to the shooting a large number of black students had been carrying guns on campus and that there was a great deal of fear and tension. A meeting was called in Campbel Hall on January 19 to try to smooth over the disagreements about the appointment of a new director and to achieve solidarity within the Black Students Union. As John Jerome Huggins, 23, and Al Prentice (Bunchy) Carter, 26, local Black Panther leaders, left the meeting on the first floor of Campbell Hall, guns were drawn, and both were fatally shot. Law enforcement personnel descended on the scene, and the assailants were located fairly quickly. Three High Potential students, who were apparently affiliated with US—George Steiner, 22, his brother Larry, 21, and Donald Hawkins, 20—were convicted of murder in September 1969 and sentenced to life imprisonment.

This shooting and the subsequent revolutionary tone of some black leaders caused many black students to drop further participation in the center program. Shortly after the shooting, the university supported a retreat for black students at which they got a chance to pull themselves together.

The problems of the Afro-American Studies Center since the spring of 1969 have centered around leadership, shortage of black faculty, and whether a separate Department of Black Studies should be inaugurated on the UCLA campus. Robert Singleton, a member of the business administration faculty and a doctoral candidate, was appointed interim director of the center in April 1969, and in the summer of 1970 Arthur Smith, professor of speech, was appointed director. Leroy Higgenbottom, who had devised and taught an innovative program for urban internships at the School of Architecture, was appointed assistant director. Now that the center has strong leadership that is well accepted by the academic community, it has an excellent chance of making rapid progress.

Among the accomplishments of the Afro-American Studies Center in its first year of operation (1969–70) were holding a Black History Week, establishing courses in black studies that lead to a major, compiling bibliographies and a library in the field of black studies, and conducting a series of programs. The Black Students

Union put out a newspaper, *Nommo,* but it too has been plagued by controversy. In January 1970, the editors, Edward Maddox and Paul Montgomery, resigned because they wanted to be "objective news reporters rather than proponents of socialist revolution."

The center has a new set of goals in research, curriculum development, and cultural programs. It will stress black development, or the training of black leadership and technical capacity. It is hoped that the center will have a close relationship to the black community of Los Angeles and will become an agent on campus for securing the goals of the black community. The center also publishes the *Journal of Black Studies.*

The Chicano Cultural Center At the end of the summer of 1970, the Chicano Cultural Center was still without a full-time "academically qualified" director, but it had been headed for a year by a capable administrative coordinator, Gil Garcia. The three principal thrusts of the center have been in putting out a journal, forging ties with Chicano communities, and assisting departments to recruit Mexican-American faculty. A proposed Chicano studies program has been hampered by the fact that, as of the academic year 1969–70, there were only two Chicano faculty members, and they have been able to offer only two courses.

Gil Garcia was extremely critical of the university for not giving enough financial support to the center and for being slow to refurbish the center headquarters. His principal complaint, however, was about the inherent conservatism and elitism of university faculty members:

We are dealing with a group of people who represent the Establishment, and think they are morally, intellectually and racially superior to us. This dehumanizing process will eventually permeate all the members of this society in order for these elite, self-appointed, high priest, senile, assinine, igoramus, chrome-plated garbage cans to rule and never be challenged.

Balancing the animosity he feels toward the administration is Garcia's extreme pride in the solidarity of the Chicano students. He feels that he, the faculty members, and the students can move the administration if they stick together and demand what is needed to make the center function. The center has worked hard to raise the image of Mexican-Americans. Its journal, *Aztlan* (Chicano Journal of the Social Sciences and the Arts), is a first-rate publication, in English, with striking artwork, challenging and scholarly articles, and a proud tone. The center is adorned with Mexican-

American artifacts and art, presenting a bright contrast to most of grimy Campbell Hall. Garcia and the students have accomplished a great deal.

The Chicano Cultural Center has been deeply involved in the community. The Centro Universitario was established through the UCLA Extension Division to provide education in the Chicano community, using Chicano students from the center. However, because of uncertainty about its success and general fund cutbacks throughout the University of California, the program was curtailed. Mexican-American students worked with the Law School to secure the funding for La Casa Legal de Los Angeles (the Legal House of Los Angeles) to supply legal services to the Chicano community. Chicano students have also been involved in tutoring in the community as part of the Teen Opportunities Program.

Perhaps the most significant thing about the center is the fact that a prestigious and powerful institution such as UCLA has come out on the side of Chicano culture and self-pride.

The American Indian Center

In many ways, the center for Native Americans is the slowest of the four to get off the ground. It did not get its first full-time director until Anthony Purley was appointed to the post in the summer of 1970. The American Indian Center faced more difficult problems than the other three, because there were almost no Native American faculty and students at UCLA, and there was a shortage of potential faculty for recruitment.

Until Purley's appointment, the center mainly attempted to recruit Indian students to the university and provided support to them once they enrolled.

Anthony Purley's background was in industry, where he worked on federal poverty programs involving Indians. He is plugged in to the new American Indian leadership, which stresses self-determination and pride.

As of the summer of 1970, the goals of the center were fairly indeterminate, but there was a general service orientation. There is a plan to tie the university to an Indian boarding school to show how such a school can be improved with proper management and resources.

The Asian-American Studies Center

The Asian-American Studies Center has differed from the others in several respects. Its members have a variety of ethnic backgrounds, including Japanese, Chinese, and Filipino ancestry. Only the Filipinos could be considered disadvantaged from an educational and economic point of view. Although the Asian-Americans are the largest minority group at UCLA, they are also the least organized and the most apathetic, in part because most of them have been doing fairly well. The center has suffered from not having a full-time director and from having a less focused program.

Nevertheless a small number of Asian-American students have been deeply involved in the center. They have evolved a variety of community programs, including a free university in Chinatown, teaching English as a second language to new immigrants, and tutoring programs. Some research is under way, but it is difficult to determine what shape this will take.

There is a feeling of dissatisfaction on the part of the students. An article on the center in the UCLA newspaper, the *Daily Bruin,* in February 1970, was highly critical of the administration and noted that the center had succeeded in buying off the militant Asian-Americans while the rest remained apathetic.

Colin Watnaaba, an Asian student involved with and extremely critical of the center, felt that the principal purpose of ethnic studies should be to revolutionize the educational system:

You can't start new things while the University is still straitjacketed in its orientation to turning out degrees. We started Ethnic Studies and it ended up just like a regular University course—that's why many people see it as a dead end thing. The goal is to change the institutions of the society and also the people of the society. When we talk about doing this in the University framework, it's too limited a framework.

The associate director of the center, Yuji Ichioka, felt that the center had very little power because administration checks restrict the scope of its activities. "In setting up these programs, the University hasn't changed structurally. We cannot hire faculty; we cannot teach courses ourselves; nor can we grant a degree."

Future Expansion There have already been spin-offs from the ethnic centers themselves. One of the most interesting was the UCLA program of ethnic studies in Venice, California (a nearby, run-down community), during the summer of 1969, in which both Mexican-American history and Afro-American history were taught by college students to high school students. Eight instructors taught 12 courses. The goal was not just to impart ethnic information but also to build a sense of self-pride and to interest the students in going to college. Both the high school students who took the classes and the undergraduate and graduate students who had to prepare and deliver the courses got a great deal out of the program. As the ethnic centers grow and become stronger, a variety of such cooperative center community service projects should become possible.

THE ADMINISTRA-TION'S VIEW OF THE PROGRAM David Saxon, the vice-chancellor of the university, summed up his reaction to the early life of the ethnic centers by stating that they had done about as well as could have been expected but not as well as he would have liked. Certainly no one could have foreseen the conflict and controversy that have touched each of the centers. Although the administration has been criticized by representatives of all four centers, it provided adequate space and substantial funding (in the neighborhood of $½million for the academic year 1970–71).

Vice-Chancellor Wilson feels clearly that the centers should develop as the ethnic minorities who will be served by them desire and not according to a blueprint emanating from the administration. He is pleased by the important role students have played in each of the centers. He is hopeful that, now that the students have played the major role in getting the centers going, the faculty will see their potential and will become deeply involved, as has been the case in the Afro-American Studies Center.

Although the centers have been plagued by problems and are at present far from perfect, they offer an excellent model for applying pressure to the university for change from within. If the administration had been less sure of itself and had not had public funding, the program would probably never have been started in the first place and certainly would not have been continued in the face of the difficulty and controversy encountered.

References

Cross, Alison: "Asian Studies Here 'Buys Off Militants': Others Apathetic," *UCLA Daily Bruin,* Feb. 12, 1970.

Kitano, Harry, and Dorothy Miller: *An Assessment of Educational Opportunity Programs in California Higher Education,* Scientific Analysis Corporation, San Francisco, 1970. (Mimeographed.)

Rhodes, Barbara: *UCLA High Potential Program: 1968–1969,* University of California, Los Angeles, 1970. (Mimeographed.)

Weiler, Daniel, and Miles Rogers: *The UCLA Educational Opportunities Program: 1964–1968,* (A "Technical Memorandum" Report), Systems Development Corporation, Santa Monica, Calif., 1969.

5. Our Lady of the Lake: A Different Type of Service

Although Our Lady of the Lake (The Lake), a medium-size, predominantly women's Catholic college in San Antonio, Texas, has always had a variety of distinctive programs, it has still hewed fairly close to tradition. The great majority of the undergraduates are Catholic. Catholic students are still required to take one religion course. Many of the parents send their daughters there with the feeling that they will be protected from the dangers of the outside world.

In 1967, The Lake began a radical experiment called Project Teacher Excellence (PTE), which enrolled Mexican-American students who would not ordinarily qualify for admission to or be able to afford the school. The project aimed to prepare them to become bilingual teachers in the Mexican-American community. This has been a bold experiment, fraught with difficulty, but it is succeeding because of the support of key faculty members and administrators and the tremendous ability of the students themselves. Its success has made PTE's supporters and students proud and has caused many of its original detractors to rethink their opposition. Project Teacher Excellence has also had an impact on other units at The Lake; for example, a dean at the Worden School of Social Service said, "If they can do it, why can't we?" Although PTE has been a success to date, its long-range future is by no means secure.

This chapter tells the story of Project Teacher Excellence, the conflicts that it has engendered, why it has succeeded, and how it has affected the rest of the college.

BACKGROUND OF THE COMMUNITY San Antonio has one of the largest concentrations of Mexican-American population of any major city in the United States. Today approximately 40 percent of its 800,000 citizens are Mexican-American, and in the future they are expected to be a majority.

59

(Mexican-Americans also refer to themselves as "Chicanos" and "browns." However, those of Mexican descent in Texas seem to prefer to be called Mexican-Americans, and that is the term I shall use throughout.)

The most acute educational problem in the Southwest concerns the education of Mexican-American children. In the elementary and secondary schools of the five states in the region—Arizona, California, Colorado, New Mexico, and Texas—there are approximately 1,750,000 children with Spanish surnames. Approximately two-thirds of the public school population of San Antonio is Mexican-American. The statistics on the children's performance are abysmal. Only a small proportion go to college. Because of this, school-teachers are predominantly white (Anglo), and many of them have been ineffective in reaching and motivating Mexican-American students.

THE NATURE OF THE COLLEGE Our Lady of the Lake is located on the west side of San Antonio, in a predominantly Mexican-American, low-income part of town. This location is one reason the upper-middle-class Catholic girls of San Antonio usually attend Trinity University rather than The Lake. The Lake's Anglo resident students have been primarily Catholic girls from north and east Texas and out of state. The college has long had a substantial population of middle- and working-class Mexican-American students commuting from the San Antonio area, whose parents, through economizing, have been able to afford the tuition of $750 a year.

Service to the community has been a major component of The Lake's program since it was founded by the Sisters of the Divine Providence as a two-year Catholic college in 1911. Teacher training has always been a major activity.

The Lake is a fairly strong college academically, and over the years it has raised its entrance requirements. By 1968, two-thirds of the entering freshmen came from the top quarter of their graduating classes in high school. Financial and academic considerations ruled out many Mexican-Americans. Before Project Teacher Excellence enrolled its first students in September 1967, the college had done little to educate poorly prepared students.

Project Teacher Excellence was not a program that sprang up overnight in barren soil. There was a context at The Lake that made such innovation possible. The Sisters of Divine Providence established the first normal school in Texas at San Antonio, and it eventually became Our Lady of the Lake. The Worden School of Social Service was the first in San Antonio.

However, much of the service rendered to the community by the sisters in the early days was of the "Lady Bountiful" nature. The sisters contributed baskets of food to local residents at Thanksgiving. According to some younger Mexican-Americans, the community regarded The Lake as a patronizing mission surrounded by high fences, which was inaccessible to most of the poor children who lived nearby. The college administrators have become aware of this image and have started to change it. Some sisters now live in low-income Mexican-American communities, and this has helped to change perspectives on both sides.

The seeds of today's innovations were sown by a self-study The Lake made in preparation for an accreditation visit in the 1960s. The administrators determined that service to the community would be an important goal. The first step was a visit by two sisters (who were eventually to become the second- and third-ranking administrators at The Lake) to a number of other colleges. The sisters were particularly impressed by Antioch, Carleton, Macalester, and Webster, and they became convinced of the importance of faculty and student involvement in policy making.

Joint faculty-student committees now make most of the important decisions at The Lake. Because the students were fairly conservative, they had to be urged and cajoled to serve on committees. At first, students could not see what relevance tenure appointments had for them. Traditionally the faculty was ahead of the students in liberalization at The Lake, until the arrival of the Project Teacher Excellence students.

Although The Lake now admits academically underqualified students and is going coeducational, it is still conservative. The music piped into the dining room and the posters hung in the corridors contain little hint of the revolution that is going on within higher education. The buildings are traditional. The faculty and students dress conservatively. The alumni are a major force inhibiting innovation. (Four alumni called The Lake to protest an appearance of folk singer Pete Seeger.) The Lake is a conservative institution compared to Wayne State or Northeastern, but fairly radical for a Catholic college. Perhaps its conservatism is best described by one of its top administrators:

... I would be the first to admit that OLL has a conservative element on its campus (we would not be much of a forum for the free flow of ideas if we systematically excluded the conservative point of view), but Dr. Nash seems to find this conservatism omnipresent and all-powerful, and I simply cannot buy this interpretation. . . . The official planning report of the Steering Committee on Development, which will serve as the master plan for the next ten years, is hardly a timid backward-looking document in its projections for student body mix, for radical curricular reform, and for program innovations. . . .

I submit that any slowness in responding to innovation is . . . a result of the financial squeeze in which all higher educational institutions are being caught. . . . No responsible administrator encourages the initiation of a program or project, unless some reasonable planning can also be done for the providing of resources for that program or project. The reason for the success of the projects that OLL has undertaken is that they were not half-baked ideas emerging from nowhere, but carefully (and perhaps slowly) thought out objectives that could be carried out on the limited resources available to a small private college.

PROJECT TEACHER EXCELLENCE In 1963 Harold Wren, the chairman of the education department, conceived the idea for Project Teacher Excellence. It was to take Mexican-American students who would not normally have been eligible for admission to college and train them to become teachers in their own communities. Wren originally wanted $900,000 for a five-year project. His proposal was sent to the Office of Economic Opportunity, which kept it for some time. Finally OEO told Our Lady of the Lake to resubmit the proposal to the Office of Education, as that was the appropriate funding source. Guy Pryor, a professor of education, promptly resubmitted the proposal, but it was turned down by the Office of Education. In December 1966, some months after submission of the second proposal, Tom Jones, a special assistant to Secretary of Health, Education, and Welfare John Gardner, came across The Lake's proposal when Gardner asked him to review promising proposals for the education of Mexican-Americans that had been rejected. Jones met with college administrators to discuss a further resubmission of the proposal.

Jones explained that the project had been turned down not because of lack of merit but because it did not correspond to existing programs funded by the Office of Education. Again the proposal was submitted, and again it was turned down because it still did not correspond closely enough to anything offered by the Office of Education.

Because Secretary Gardner and the Office of Mexican-American

Affairs in the Office of Education were still interested, Dave Johnson, head of the Office of Education's Talent Search Program, became interested in the program. The Talent Search Program stretched its regulations and awarded $40,000 to Our Lady of the Lake for a two-year period, for locating and recruiting students for the program.

The basic funding for the program was then secured through three federal financial aid programs of the Office of Education: the Educational Opportunity Grant program, the College Work-Study program, and the National Defense Student Loan program. The budget for these three programs at Our Lady of the Lake in 1970–71 was to be approximately $800,000 with a very large proportion of that money going to the PTE students. The college has also provided scholarships, and federal guaranteed loans have been secured through the Texas Opportunity Program. The Southwest Educational Development Laboratories gave $20,000 assistance to the program at the outset. In addition, Our Lady of the Lake, St. Mary's College, and the Model Cities program have secured an additional $160,000 per year from the Special Services for the Disadvantaged program of the Office of Education. These funds will pay for tutoring and academic makeup work, for which no money was previously available. The Talent Search Program has been continued and is now called Puerta Abierta for Economically Deprived and Culturally Differentiated Americans.

The Lake has been able to operate Project Teacher Excellence at the rate it envisioned, bringing in 40 students per year since the fall of 1967, with the funds provided by the federal government. However, it had to adapt its request for funds to existing programs, rather than getting money in the form it had originally proposed. It was not until personal relationships were established with program administrators in the Office of Education that people at The Lake were able to figure out how to proceed.

The Performance of the Project

Of the students who were admitted to the project during the first year, 60 percent did not qualify for admission to Our Lady of the Lake by the usual standards for admission, yet the project group had a smaller percentage of failures and a smaller percentage on scholastic probation than did the freshman class as a whole. By the end of the third year of the project, in the spring of 1970, 85 percent of all enrollees in the program since its inception were still enrolled in it at The Lake. Of those who dropped out, one-third transferred to other colleges. Only 10 percent of those who entered the program have not continued in college. Some of those who transferred were unhappy with The Lake itself. Some were men who decided against teaching, and there was no other program for them at The Lake then. As of the spring of 1970, there were approximately 1,000 full-time undergraduates at The Lake. Of these, about 50 percent were Mexican-American and 6 percent black. The PTE students constituted about one-quarter of the Mexican-American student body.

Despite the fact that the retention rate has been high, the grades of students in the program have been somewhat lower than average. The PTE students encountered tremendous problems; the administrators of the program and the individual attention given have kept the students enrolled. The most frequent troubles have arisen from the students' poor foundations in English, their cultural conflicts over the value of higher education, and mechanical impediments such as transportation problems or illness in the family.

The Central Characters

The story of The Lake cannot be understood without reference to three key figures in the administration and faculty. The two top-ranking sisters were responsible for creating a climate at The Lake that made innovation possible and for offering crucial support at the many times when Project Teacher Excellence encountered rough going.

Betty Carrow was the Lake's only vice-president and in charge of development, public relations, and planning before she left the college and the sisterhood in the summer of 1969. She and Sister Mary Clare Metz, the academic dean, were the two sisters who provided The Lake's real leadership, both in faculty involvement and in community projects. Betty Carrow was unusual in that she had a Ph.D. in speech therapy from Northwestern University, a non-Catholic institution. When she returned to The Lake from Northwestern, she organized the Harry Jersig Speech and Hearing Center, which now has a new building and a staff of 15 professionals.

Betty Carrow is a competent, attractive, progressive, friendly person. Although she was not involved in starting Project Teacher Excellence, she was an important factor in The Lake's other areas of community involvement: the Model Cities program, the Salute to Mexico program, the proposed creative arts center, and almost everything else that was new or innovative. She left The Lake and the sisterhood to become a professor at the Baylor School of Medicine, partly because she felt that the constant conflicts between the forces for change and against change were not resolvable within the existing structure. Although she won most of the battles she fought, what she remembers most is the tremendous struggle that was required to bring about change.

Sister Mary Clare Metz, the academic dean, got her Ph.D. in biology from Catholic University, after graduating from The Lake. Her gray hair and her dress-length habit are stylish, and her demeanor is forceful but pleasant and optimistic at the same time. She was a strong force at The Lake because she was traditional enough to be accepted by the conservatives and because she is extremely reasonable.

Guy Pryor, a professor of education, has been the father of the PTE program since its inception. He is a white Protestant, pushing sixty, who has been characterized as being "as liberal as a professional educator from Texas can be." He has been unswerving in his support for the PTE program and can talk endlessly about it in a most positive fashion. He has established really good communication and relations with the PTE students, and he and they pride themselves on his proper pronunciation of their names. He is firm but warm and friendly with the students and fights for their causes when he thinks something needs to be corrected.

When the students were unhappy about the financial aid officer, they went to see President McMahon. McMahon told Pryor, "I'm looking to you to keep the peace." Pryor responded, "You can't expect me to keep from reporting injustice. If anything happens on this campus in the way of disorder, it will be the fault of the administration for not correcting injustices and not the fault of students who are protesting it." Pryor and his program have enough acceptance on campus and academic freedom is sufficiently respected for him to be outspoken without risk.

Pryor knows each of the PTE students and does not hesitate to be firm with them. "I'm not tough; I just tell them the facts of life. I can't be expected to battle to keep them out of academic trouble if they don't attend class. That's just telling them the facts of life."

The students are very positive about Pryor and are not afraid to be outspoken in his presence about anything they do not like. He regarded it as his greatest compliment when one of them said: "Dr. Pryor, you're a real Mexican."

The Program The PTE program revolves around four components:

1 *Bilingual education,* the philosophical foundation of the program, an ideology that has shaped much of the students' attitudes and behavior

2 *The recruitment of Mexican-American students with lower socioeconomic backgrounds* who would not normally have been qualified for admission to The Lake and who have a commitment to teaching

3 *Financial aid* to enable these students from low-income backgrounds to attend The Lake and in many cases to live on campus

4 *Academic guidance* and responsibility for the program, emanating from the office of Guy Pryor

The Project Teacher Excellence program has not resulted in a vastly revised curriculum. There have been unsuccessful efforts to start a Mexican-American Studies program. Prior to 1970 there was no organized remedial or tutoring program. The college's grant under the Special Services for the Disadvantaged program should enable PTE to offer a different curriculum, especially for beginning students. However, because of poor high school preparation, many of the PTE students have to work harder than their classmates, and this has resulted in considerable extra work for faculty members as well.

Bilingual education
Project Teacher Excellence is based on the idea that Mexican-Americans have a unique capacity to teach Mexican-American school children—especially in the early grades. Bilingual education might more properly be called "bicultural" education or "education without denigration."

Bilingual education starts with the assumption that the child with a different background from the middle-class, white, Protestant child who predominates in the American public school is not as much deprived as he is different. Public schools have been run for the white, middle-class majority. This need not prevent a child from a different culture from being appreciated, made to feel comfortable, and aided in adapting to a new culture.

Because Mexican-American teachers understand and appreciate the culture of their pupils, and because they can communicate easily in Spanish (not the classical type, but the variety spoken by Mexican-Americans in Texas), they have the greatest potential for reaching Mexican-American children. Furthermore, they are excellent role models. The Project Teacher Excellence graduates offer young Mexican-American students the most visible proof that they, too, can make it.

The students have one important problem with Mexican-American culture that programs like Project Teacher Excellence should help to overcome. With one another, Mexican-Americans are proud of their culture, but they tend to be ashamed of it in front of white Americans because they know it is looked down on. One PTE girl who grew up in a predominantly non-Mexican-American neighborhood described the reaction thus: "We used to love tacos and eat them all the time. But if an anglo came to the door, the first thing mother would say would be 'Hide the tacos; it's an anglo.' "

Recruitment into PTE

Recruitment has not been a problem. The Talent Search Program staff established the right contacts to reach the students for whom the program was intended. Students were accepted on a very personal basis. The program aimed to get people who could succeed in college but had not necessarily demonstrated it. The selection criteria were cited in the first report on PTE by the program's staff:

Financial Need is a prerequisite for selection.

Academic Ability, even though possibly below usual standards, must be evident sufficiently to indicate some possibility of success in college. Outstanding academic ability is neither sought nor discounted.

The *Motivational Factors* and *Personal Qualities* are plus factors that enable the applicant to emerge from among his competitors for selection.

Admissions decisions were made by the PTE office and not by the college admissions office.

Financial aid

The three Office of Education financial aid programs have been the principal support of the PTE program. Many college and financial aid officers operate on the presumption that students should be given only a part of the money they need and encouraged to "scratch" for the rest. Early in the program, Guy Pryor determined that this would not work. There was no place for these poor students to scratch. Consequently, a decision was made to give the students full financial support, including a modest stipend for spending money.

Conflicts with the former director of financial aid caused the most severe crisis in the project's history. According to the PTE staff, the sister who administered financial aid had an excellent mind for detail but caused the students immense problems by her method of dealing with them. Some students felt that she looked down on them and acted as if she were doling out charity. Eventually she was replaced by a competent Mexican-American man.

Because the story is complex and controversial and because personalities are involved, I will quote a summary of the situation by an administrator who was close to the scene:

The Sister who was financial aid officer was basically a good person who was steeped in the tradition of dispensing financial aid as charity. Her lack of cultural understanding, inconsistent and inequitable decisions, poor student relationships, and lack of vision for the potential of properly administered financial aid, caused her to be an impediment to the continuation of PTE. Her transfer to more suitable endeavors and the employment of a more flexible person with a broader concept of financial aid enabled the project to get back on even keel and expand. The low morale of the students disappeared. Her transfer was aided by some, resisted by some, and delayed by inaction. But the institution, after great travail, moved forward with a program of financial aid that gives an opportunity for poverty students to be successful in college.

Two interesting conclusions can be drawn from the problems caused by the original financial aid officer. The first is that the individual's personality and method of operation can be just as important as what he does. Secondly, the difficulty that the administration had in resolving the situation and the slowness with which it moved were indicative of the problems that institutions of higher education have in dealing with urban and minority problems.

Direction and guidance

Guy Pryor's intense interest in the students has been a major factor in keeping them in the program and helping them to succeed. The PTE staff and key faculty and administrators have made a point of getting to know the students as people and of helping them to solve their personal problems, no matter how mundane or minute. This is especially important for students who would not normally have come to college and who cannot depend on family or friends for support and advice. Now that the program has been going for several years, the older students have taken over much of the guidance work that the PTE staff originally had to do. The program also benefited by taking in upperclassmen as transfer students, as well as freshmen, so that the original PTE students included some with more maturity.

One of the typical reactions of the PTE students was avoidance. Pryor found that when the students had problems, they frequently became ashamed, as well as disturbed, and stopped attending classes. When they seemed upset or started cutting classes, they were called in. One girl went to pieces because she was unable to complete a term paper on time. Pryor arranged for an extension on her paper and listened patiently while she told the tearful story of her problem. All she needed was someone to talk to and to give her a little advice and help; then she managed well on her own.

Effects on and of the Students

From the beginning, a strong esprit de corps emerged among the students. The PTE students are the largest faction on campus, and by using modern organizing procedures they have come to dominate the student government. They have protested about conditions and caused changes, where the apathetic majority had been displeased but had not known how to take action.

The program has been willing to take chances on various types of people and to show real concern for all the people it has admitted. One of the most impressive students is Adelpha Galvan, a girl who has poor hearing, poor eyesight, and a speech defect. She just barely made it out of high school and was told by her high school counselor not to apply to college.

Miss Galvan came for a personal interview and was accepted as a PTE student because of her motivation. The Lake has provided her with speech therapy and a hearing aid. In addition to her other problems, she was hit by a truck, while on a student march to raise funds for tuberculosis, and was hospitalized with a broken pelvis. The college made arrangements to have all her classes meet in one classroom with a bed in it, so that she could keep up with her course work. Miss Galvan will probably become an outstanding teacher. Her case illustrates a principal advantage of the small college: students are known to the faculty and administration and can receive individual solutions to their problems.

There has been a clash of cultures between the PTE girls and the other students. Most of the previous students, whether Anglos or

Mexican-Americans, were middle-class ladies. The PTE girls were more boisterous, less restrained, and much more willing to be critical of the college. The first day that one of the girls wore a miniskirt, three different sisters told her that her appearance was not appropriate at Our Lady of the Lake. Another girl was criticized for dating too many different boys.

The PTE students were the first to voice strong objection to some of the courses. Carmen Prieto, an early graduate of the program, said: "We were all peeved with the Social Theory course. We all had to suffer and we all got C's. The Community course was a complete waste of time. The teacher said something about theory but she didn't know anything at all about San Antonio." Miss Prieto was annoyed that the task of bringing about change had fallen to the PTE students. "Before us, the good ladies just played the game. We were the only ones who spoke out."

Many changes have been made in a variety of courses since the Project Teacher Excellence girls started to complain. One course that has been completely revamped is Ethnic Relations. A new professor has brought in outside speakers and movies, and the students feel that the course has improved markedly.

Changes came about because PTE students complained, and faculty and staff responded. The PTE staff was the crucial link in the chain. Guy Pryor listened to the complaints and carried them to faculty and administration.

OTHER COMMUNITY INVOLVEMENT EFFORTS Our Lady of the Lake has become involved in the Mexican-American community in a number of other ways since the start of Project Teacher Excellence. None of them has been as effective as PTE. However, all the efforts combined give The Lake a substantial across-the-board involvement with the Mexican-American community.

The Model Cities Program The office for the Model Cities program in the area near the college was located in college quarters. According to Henry Cisnero, the assistant director of San Antonio Model Cities, the college was extremely cooperative in providing space for staff, parking, and meeting rooms. Substantively, The Lake became involved on the education and housing committees, and the School of Social Work participated in a number of projects. Such involvement is no guarantee that the college will earn good marks from the community. Cisnero was frustrated by The Lake's conservatism. He reflected:

The Lake is an ivory tower in a state of turmoil over conflicting concepts of its being a finishing school and its being an involved place. Project Teacher Excellence is tearing up the place. Before Project Teacher Excellence, the student body, including the Mexican-Americans, were nice, Catholic, mother-protected girls. The College is at least ten years behind in doing something for the education of Mexican-Americans. . . . I'm afraid that it may go back to being a conservative institution after flirting with involvement.

Creative Arts of San Antonio (CASA) A $50,000 planning grant was obtained from the Special Opportunity Planning Section of the Department of Health, Education, and Welfare to establish CASA as an integral part of the Model Cities program. The arts center will tie together the teaching ability of the college's strong art department, the art students at the college, and the need and desire of people in the community to encourage Mexican-American art. It hopes to use art as a means by which the local residents can discover Mexican-American culture.

Salute to Mexico The Salute to Mexico program began in the spring of 1968 and has been held each year since then. It has presented ballet, concerts, and art shows. Its high-caliber program, complete with professional talent, has been a joint endeavor of the college and the cultural arm of the Mexican State Department. The aim has been to show San Antonians that Mexico has a highly developed culture.

The Worden School of Social Service Although the School of Social Service has graduated Mexican-American social workers, set up community placement centers in the barrios, served agencies dealing with Mexican-Americans, and done research on hunger and other problems of the Mexican-American community, it has still lagged behind in some areas.

There was only one Mexican-American faculty member until 1970; now another is being hired. However, the school does have 12 part-time Mexican-American "field instructors." The Lake is one of four institutions whose schools of social work are sharing a five-year grant from the National Institute of Mental Health to recruit Mexican-American faculty members and students and to revise the curriculum. Eventually the School of Social Work aims to have Mexican-American students constitute 20 percent of its enrollment. A study completed in 1969 by the National Council on Social Work showed that 12 of the 21 Mexican-Americans holding M.S.W.'s has been educated at Worden.

The School of Social Service is involved in a delinquency prevention project that is the only direct outgrowth of The Lake's involvement with the Model Cities program.

THE FUTURE OF PTE AND THE LAKE The key to The Lake's success in the future will be its ability to attract and retain high-caliber leadership and to form meaningful ties with the Mexican-American community. Innovative administrators will probably still find The Lake a frustrating place at which to work. Betty Carrow left because she felt that everything was just too much of a fight. Until people like her feel that such a college can be an exciting place, one that invites innovation, the potential of small, special colleges will not be realized. However, The Lake has done a host of exciting things, has gained confidence now in its ability to experiment, and has left most small, parochial colleges far behind.

References

Project Teacher Excellence Annual Progress Report, 1967–1968, Our Lady of the Lake College, San Antonio, Tex., 1968.

"What Does Urban America Have to Do with That Small Catholic Liberal Arts College Called 'Our Lady of the Lake'?" *Our Lady of the Lake College Magazine,* vol. 1, no. 3, pp. 1–3, November 1968.

6. Morgan State: Dedicated to Excellence and Leadership

Each of the institutions of higher education studied in this book was selected because it had made one or more serious efforts to involve itself in urban, minority, and community problems. Each was fairly innovative. My first visit to Morgan State College, a predominantly black institution in Baltimore, Maryland, led me to feel that the college was somewhat more conservative and traditional than others in our study. When I got to know Morgan State better, however, I realized that it had devised its own solutions to the problems of black people in cities and that these solutions, although different from those employed in predominantly white institutions, were appropriate and successful.

Morgan State has contributed in three distinct ways to the solution of urban, community, and minority-group problems:

1   It is a first-rate institution for black people in a white and predominantly racist society. Morgan State is a high-quality institution in every way: in its educational and athletic programs, in its imaginative responses to student demands for change, in its physical facilities, in its urban involvement, and, perhaps most important, in its administration.

2   It is an outstanding educator of black people. For 20 years Morgan State has worked hard to prepare people for leadership positions who might not otherwise have gone to college.

3   Its faculty, staff, and administrators serve in leadership positions in Baltimore and on the national scene.

Morgan State has achieved its principal successes by evolving into a quality black institution that serves black people and is an object of pride for them. It more than holds its own in the rough and tumble of competition among institutions of higher education. Only a handful of other black institutions can make the same claim.

One of the most controversial subjects at Morgan State is whether or not it should continue to be predominantly black. President Martin Jenkins wanted the college to become a truly integrated urban university serving all of Baltimore. The curriculum of the university that Jenkins envisioned would have emphasized urban problems in general and the needs of Baltimore in particular. Whether the idea could have worked will never be known, because the Maryland Council for Higher Education turned it down. Some of the black students were upset about the proposed integrated college and wanted Morgan State to remain a predominantly black experience, although the student government and a majority of students approved Jenkins's idea.

Morgan State is predominantly black, not by exclusion but because relatively few whites choose to enroll there as undergraduates, although the college has made a strong effort to recruit them. The most segregated aspect of the institution is the undergraduate student body, which, as of the fall of 1968, had less than 100 whites out of approximately 3,500 students. The graduate school is much more integrated, with approximately half of its 500 students being white. On the faculty, there is one white for every three blacks. In intercollegiate athletics, Morgan State competes with both predominantly white and predominantly black institutions. The college has also engaged in cooperative endeavors with white institutions, including the University of Pennsylvania and Johns Hopkins University.

Morgan State prides itself on leadership and excellence. The Urban Studies Institute, founded in the fall of 1963, is probably the first such institute in the country located at an undergraduate college. Project Mission, a precursor of the Teacher Corps in preparing urban teachers, was one of the first in the country. Morgan was also one of the first colleges to have a special education program for students who would not normally have been admissible.

It was the administration of the college, under the presidency of Martin Jenkins (which ended in the academic year 1969-70), that made Morgan State a model institution. Jenkins, whose businesslike and serious demeanor made him seem more like a corporate executive than a college president, worked with state, federal, and foundation officials to build Morgan State into an institution of excellence. He had a few long-range goals, and he pursued them doggedly and determinedly over the 22 years of his presidency. He is a pragmatist who forged good relationships with the political leaders upon whose support he depended, yet he never kept his opinions to himself when there were disagreements. He ran the college with a firm hand, being involved in every major decision, but he had an open-door policy with the students and won the respect of his faculty. Although modest and realistic in person, he did not hesitate to attempt to inspire. His book, *An Adventure in Higher Education,* ends with goals for both faculty and students:

> It is my desire to bring to Morgan State College teachers who are characterized by high ability and excellent academic preparation; the desire and ability to do a superior job of teaching. . . . I am convinced that any real institution must be concerned with the student as a total person . . . this contrasts with the view that teachers are concerned only with the fragmental development of students in their particular subject area. Teachers are expected to counsel with students on academic or non-academic matters; to attend occasionally at least the campus affairs given by and for students; and, if possible, to occasionally invite students to their homes. Teachers should in their own behavior and manifested interests reveal to students the characteristics of a liberally educated person . . . a real interest in the community — teachers are also citizens; teachers at this college should be good citizens. . . . (Jenkins, 1964, p. 95).

> I should like every Morgan man and woman to strive for these goals during the undergraduate years; to exhibit intellectual integrity and habits of logical and critical thinking; to read widely with understanding and enjoyment; to convey ideas in clear and concise written and oral expression; to master the techniques of learning; . . . to have the self-confidence and determination which are necessary for achievement at high levels; to be a Second Miler — to do more than is expected in any given task; to exemplify in his relations with other people honesty and integrity, a keen sense of responsibility, freedom from racial prejudices and petty social intolerances (Ibid., p. 94).

The nature of the leadership and administration at Morgan State can perhaps best be understood from a look at how reforms in student life and government were brought about. Several years ago, a group of students, including the minority white students on campus, formed an organization called Dissent that protested the compulsory nature of the Reserve Officers Training Corps (ROTC). The compulsory aspect was quickly changed, although ROTC was maintained. The students pressed for a number of other reforms, including liberalization of rules in the dormitory. These changes were also brought about fairly easily. The leaders of the student government concluded that President Jenkins did maintain an open-door policy, did listen to student grievances, and was open to change. They join him in feeling that the administration and faculty at Morgan State are ahead of the students and that the students have not become as involved in community affairs or in restructuring the college as they could have been.

Our first impression was that the education was too traditional and that the students were not getting out of the classroom and into service-learning situations enough. In large measure this pattern is due to the nature of the students, not the institution. Many of the Morgan students were poorly prepared in high school, and academic success does not come easily to them. Many students live at home, commute to college, and hold jobs that limit the time they can devote to campus and community activities.

THE COLLEGE AS AN EDUCATOR Many colleges now have open-admission, compensatory education programs, but Morgan State was one of the first, laying the groundwork in 1950. The goal of the program as stated in 1964 was:

. . . taking students who have experienced cultural deprivation and preparing them in the short span of the college experience to compete on a basis of equality with other American college graduates. This task requires teachers who believe that it can be accomplished and who have the ability to utilize both conventional and novel procedures to assure its accomplishment.

Morgan's special education program anticipated most of the developments that have since occurred in the field. It was built around flexible admissions policies with an attempt to spot motivated, capable students who had not fully realized their potential. Other ingredients were extensive scrutiny of individuals and a good deal of personal guidance. For the freshman year, students were separated into three tracks, and those who started at a disadvantage were given extensive extra course work. The compensatory education project involved a large proportion of the colleges students.

Many of the special education features instituted at prestigious liberal arts colleges like Oberlin and Swarthmore are not to be found here. Morgan State places first things first: "The College need not apologize for having as a primary objective the occupational preparation of students—for a long time to come it must play a major role in producing personnel for high-level occupations. . . ."

How Morgan's program operates may best be illustrated by examining the experience of one student. Roger Brooks did not reach his senior year at Morgan until he was in his late twenties. He had started at Morgan in his early twenties after exhibiting potential and passing the high school equivalency exam to compensate for having dropped out of high school. After two years at Morgan, he got tired of being short of money and took a job as an aide in a mental hospital. He was active in organizing a union in the hospital and liked the work, but he realized how the lack of a degree limited his potential. By the time he came back to finish at Morgan State, he was really serious about his education and got excellent grades.

Black Studies Morgan State's black studies program is academic, offering a number of courses in a variety of departments relating to both black culture and Africa. Courses include "The Traditional African Arts," "The Negro in American Prose," and "The Negro and Music." The program was inaugurated with almost no controversy and is considered outstanding. The college offers a variety of courses both on black people and culture and on urban affairs, but they are located within individual departments and there is no major in either.

Project Mission One of the impressive things about Morgan State is that it has often been ahead of its time. A case in point is Project Mission, a program to train inner-city schoolteachers. It began in 1965 and ran for four years, funded by the Ford Foundation. Morgan State initiated the idea and then enlisted the cooperation of two white colleges, Coppin State and Towson State. The program placed approximately 150 students as interns in the Baltimore city schools, and they spent their entire fourth year of college within the school setting. The interns received $135 per month and made a commitment to do two years of teaching in inner-city schools after their graduation. The program was regarded as a success and is part of a substantial emphasis on the inner city within the Department of Education.

The Work Service Community Cooperative President Jenkins conceived the idea of the Work Service Community Cooperative project to let students learn how to teach inner-city youngsters. As part of a social science course for credit, juniors and seniors work in community projects. A large number of agencies and organizations were selected as hosts, and the students were assigned in twos and threes to more than 30 of them. Originally about 50 students signed up for the course in the fall of 1968, but thereafter interest waned and the enrollment diminished sharply. It is not clear why this happened. It may have been that the program was too time-consuming. Despite high-level administrative commitment to what could have been an innovative educational program, the idea did not catch on.

Cooperative Education

Morgan State has a five-year cooperative education program, in which the student alternates between work at a major corporation such as the Ford Motor Company and study at the Morgan campus. The company then hires him after graduation. This is an excellent means of assuring that Morgan State graduates will enter the national economic mainstream.

The Urban Studies Institute

The Urban Studies Institute, founded in 1963, is similar to those at many other institutions of higher education in that it has never quite reached its potential, despite a good start and excellent leadership. Perhaps the major accomplishment of the institute was its role in facilitating a much broader Center for Urban Affairs, which Morgan began in the academic year 1970–71, with help from the state of Maryland and the Ford Foundation. Homer Favor, an economist, has headed the institute from the start. Its scope was limited by the fact that it received only $35,000 per year. As of 1969–70, there were only two professionals on the institute staff, concentrating in the areas of research, extension, and curriculum and serving as urban resources and catalysts for the rest of the college.

Most of the contract research undertaken by the Urban Studies Institute was done fairly early in its history. Among the projects were a study of Baltimore inner-city unemployment, an evaluation of a teenage mothers program, a cooperative evaluation (with the University of Pennsylvania) of Baltimore's OEO program, and a longitudinal study of an isolated black community. Several of the programs were action programs, such as the Eastern Shore Retraining Project, which attempted to upgrade low-skilled workers.

The extension activities of the Urban Studies Institute mainly centered around conferences of regional and national scope, one or more usually held each year. The subjects have included "Higher Education and the Challenge of the Urban Crisis," "The Changing Face of Unemployment Security," and "Justice, Law and Order." These have generally had outstanding speakers and been well attended.

Both the director, Homer Favor, and the former associate director, Parren Mitchell, have taught urban-related courses on campus and serve as urban technicians for the rest of the college. Perhaps the major contribution that they have made, however, is their personal involvement in the urban scene, both in the Baltimore region and on the national level. Parren Mitchell was active in political affairs and was elected to the U.S. House of Representatives in 1970.

The Institute for Political Education
The Institute for Political Education was founded in 1959 with support from the Ford Foundation. Its principal goal was to expose Morgan State students to the functioning of the political system. Ford supported the program for eight years, and it then became dormant. The principal thrust of the institute was political internships in which Morgan students worked in the offices of elected officials. These internships were considered quite successful; the only complaint was that they were too limited in number. The institute also ran a number of action projects, including community workshops for urban dwellers and mock political conventions for students on campus.

The Proposed Center for Urban Affairs
The impetus for a new urban affairs center, named for Martin Jenkins, was an angry but constructive letter he wrote to the Ford Foundation in June 1969, complaining that predominantly black colleges had not received grants for urban involvement.

The Foundation in recent years has made substantial grants to predominantly Negro colleges for programs to improve specific weaknesses and to bring some of these institutions into the mainstream of institutions of higher education. There has been no indication, however, of massive support in areas where selected, predominantly Negro colleges and universities may develop programs as effective as any in the nation. I am convinced that with ample financial support, several predominantly Negro colleges could, with racially integrated staff and students, develop really significant programs. Demonstration that some of these institutions can be in the very front ranks of American colleges and universities in the area of urban problems will be a creative contribution to our culture.

The Center for Urban Affairs will be involved in both curriculum and service. It will be a direct outgrowth of most of the urban-related activities at Morgan State over the years. The curriculum in urban affairs will be greatly strengthened. The one new unit to be established will be a Center for the Study of the Behavior of Urban Youth. The other facets of the new center will be a cooperative education centers program (a direct outgrowth of Project Mission), an ownership training institute growing out of the Baltimore Business Institute, and an urban research institute, which will be a direct expansion of the Urban Studies Institute. The new money from the state and the Ford Foundation will enable Morgan to expand and consolidate efforts that have been going on for the past 10 years and to move from a level of honest but inadequate effort to excellence on the national scene.

MORGAN STATE AS A CITIZEN AND NEIGHBOR

Morgan's location in a predominantly white residential section of northeast Baltimore has kept it from being more heavily involved in the problems of its immediate neighborhood. The college has had some impact on the practices and attitudes of its white neighbors. Morgan students forced the integration of restaurants and theaters at a local shopping center. Many students rent rooms in white households in the neighborhood. Morgan plans to expand in the near future, and this may occasion some problems. The college shows its neighborly spirit by opening its campus to Baltimore whites and blacks in large numbers. A recreation program in the summer lets inner-city black students use the athletic facilities on campus under the direction of the college coaches. The Baltimore Symphony Orchestra performs in the Morgan auditorium to predominantly white audiences.

SUMMARY

Morgan State's method of involvement is substantially different from that of the white institutions that we have described. Morgan's principal contributions have been as an educator of black student leadership and as an institution supporting a predominantly black experience in which black people can take pride. Although this description tends to sound somewhat patronizing, this quality of the college makes it the exception rather than the rule for public institutions.

Morgan State is an excellent college that happens to be predominantly black. Its success was in large measure the result of a forceful, but constructive and pragmatic, course steered by Martin Jenkins until the fall of 1970. Jenkins, his trustees, the faculty, the staff, and the students demanded their fair share of support from public and private funding sources and documented the fact that they used such funding wisely and imaginatively. Morgan's strategies offer an example to all state-supported insitutions, which too often fail to demand support or to obtain the leadership to innovate wisely.

In describing Morgan State's position in American society today, Jenkins concludes:

In view of the temper of the times, I suspect that it is asking too much of white liberals and black activists to regard colleges attended largely by black students as American institutions of higher education rather than black institutions of higher education. I like to think that Morgan State College makes a significant contribution to the total society and that the proportion of whites in the graduate program and the faculty has a great deal of significance.

References

Baltimore City Public Schools: *Project Mission: A Cooperative Teacher Training Program for Preparing Teachers for Assignments in Inner-city Schools,* 1965. (Mimeographed.)

Jenkins, Martin D.: *An Adventure in Higher Education,* Morgan State College Press, Baltimore, 1964.

7. Northeastern University: A Private University Serving the Urban Proletariat

by Dan Waldorf

Northeastern University in Boston is something of an exception in this era of the high-tuition, high-cost, private university. Northeastern is a private university, but it has striven, since its beginning in 1898, to educate those persons who need it most but can afford it least—the poor, working-class students. It has accomplished this through its cooperative work-study plan.

COOPERATIVE EDUCATION Northeastern and the University of Cincinnati were the first universities to establish cooperative education programs. Cincinnati initiated the idea in 1906, and Northeastern took it up three years later in 1909. The program began in the College of Engineering and was subsequently adopted over the years in most of the colleges and departments of the university as they were funded and developed. Not only does the co-op program allow Northeastern to serve urban working-class students, but also much of the curriculum is geared to the urban scene.

Most recently, the Northeastern Law School went cooperative, the first law school in the United States to do so. It is also attempting a revised curriculum that eschews the usual "establishment law" in favor of more problem-oriented issues. Dean Thomas J. O'Toole summarized these efforts:

We're into conscientious objection and drug abuse. We moved a whole class into an abortion trial. Students spend a night at a police station book desk . . . and last, but not least, we even let women into our law school. We made a special pitch to women's colleges and we got them. Twenty-five percent of the 92 students are women.

Presently the cooperative scheme embraces all day students at Northeastern—approximately 13,500—and is considered by the university to be the best way to provide both education and work experience to the student population it serves.

According to Roy Wooldridge, vice-president and dean of cooperative education, Northeastern is one of the largest of 210 universities and colleges in the United States that have cooperative programs. He expects a boom in the growth of cooperatives and feels that the number will double within a few years. The idea is, according to Dean Wooldridge, politically safe: Democrats see it as a good way to educate the poor; Republicans see it as a means of cutting the costs of higher education and avoiding a federal subsidy.

Aside from the built-in payoffs of a cooperative program—providing meaningful work in a field of interest, earned income, and education—there is a hidden agenda: innovation in curriculum. The faculty is forced to change the curriculum to meet the demands of students based on experience. Cooperative work-study programs also help students develop self-confidence, provide role models of practitioners, and open the door for fund raising by the university. All these help the university determine the needs of and provide services to its local community.

Very briefly, the cooperative education program at Northeastern is a program of alternative terms of full-time work and full-time study. After a freshman year at the university, the student is placed in a job related to his major field—pharmacists in pharmaceutical jobs and physical education majors in education and recreation.

The biggest problem is in placing liberal arts, nonscience majors. These students quite often do not have specific occupational goals or are in the process of shopping around for the work they want to do. Placements for such students are less often related to the specific area of study than are those in other majors.

The job placements are intended to be broader and more meaningful than a mere work experience and are very definitely part of the education program. Supervision is provided by both the university and the employer. Continuity of placement is encouraged, but is contingent on the student's experience, likes, and dislikes.

An example of a particularly good placement was the experience of Jim Alexander, an articulate black student in the School of Journalism. During the spring of 1969, Alexander was placed with *The Christian Science Monitor* as a journalist. After a few weeks of rather routine writing jobs, he was assigned to Ford Hall at Brandeis University during the black students' take-over of that building. Students occupied the building for a week, and Alexander was the only one of many newsmen who could get in to get the black students' point of view. He got the story, did a good job writing it, and was given a by-line on the front page of the newspaper. As a result of these articles he was given a regular assignment on urban affairs and contributed several articles on black student activities, some of which appeared on the front page, again under his own by-line.

All the jobs are by no means as good or as interesting as either the students or the university would like. They are not always the learning experience the university wants them to be; frequently business and industry do not know how to use placements to best advantage, and often the employer does not provide enough supervision.

COMMUNITY INVOLVEMENT PROJECTS   The cooperative scheme sets the tone for most of the community activities at Northeastern. It provides, at the same time, relationships with local business and industry and avenues for jobs and social mobility to the working-class persons of the community.

The general feeling at Northeastern, among some of its most severe critics, the black students, is that the university is doing a good job of meeting local community needs and providing services. One student commented:

> There is no university in the country that's doing what Northeastern is doing. Like we [black student groups] didn't ask for the Lighted School House or the Dropout School; they got started on their own. But it's not like we're going to give them a lot of publicity for it; we don't want them to rest on their laurels.

In looking at Northeastern's other areas of urban, community, and minority-group involvement, it should be kept in mind that the co-op program was the lever that opened the door.

The Dropout School   The Laboratory School of the Boston Neighborhood Youth Corps, known informally as the Dropout School, began in February 1966, with active assistance from Melvin Howards, a thin, wiry, ex-New Yorker. The initial plan was to develop a modest tutorial program for Neighborhood Youth Corps workers in Roxbury, the black community of Boston. The program took a year to get funded, after several false starts and considerable disappointment. Eventually people involved became annoyed with the drawn-out funding procedures and went directly to ABCD, the Boston Community Action Program, demanding financial help to get the program going. In turn ABCD went to the Department of Labor and got money to start the program.

With funding, classes were opened on the ground floor of the YMCA, and 30 persons were initially brought into the program. During the second year, enrollment increased to 250, but during the third (and last) year of the program, it eased back to 200.

The Laboratory School provided eight hours of instruction a week to school dropouts participating in the Neighborhood Youth Corps. The major purpose of this program was

. . . to provide youth who have dropped out of school with either basic education (for those functioning below 7th grade level) or high school level work for those who have completed the 8th grade and who are functioning above the 7th grade level. Employability is the goal of the Neighborhood Youth Corps and therefore this directly affects the school program and philosophy. . . . The vast majority of the students seek better jobs with a future.

Classes were organized in track and core groups. Track groups were six to eight boys or girls grouped according to reading level, ability in English, or ability in mathematics. Only those functioning below seventh-grade levels were placed in track groups. Students who functioned above a seventh-grade level were organized into core groups of 20 persons.

Both groups had a modified curriculum for high school credit — English language, reading, mathematics, and science — organized around an integrated core concept such as conflict, migration, people who made America, getting a job, starting a bank account, or applying for a loan.

Attendance at the school was very high — 75 percent of the students attended regularly. Relationships between students and teachers were said to be "one of the best things about the school." The atmosphere was so accepting and helpful that girls with infant children often brought them to school, making arrangements among themselves and with other students for babysitting. Teachers were enthusiastic about the program, and the principal was a "very able and outspoken" black man who gave the school dynamic leadership.

Graduates of the program were successful in getting either jobs or further education. By January 1969, 29 persons had graduated from the school; of that number, 4 were full-time students at universities in the area, 5 had applied for and were awaiting admission to full-time college study, 5 were in some job training, and 9 were working full time.

The school ran for 3½ years as a demonstration project. With legislative cutbacks and changes in the Neighborhood Youth Corps guidelines during 1969, the program first had to exclude eighteen-year-olds and then was closed completely for lack of funds.

The Charles E. Mackey Lighted School House

During my first visit to Northeastern in March 1969, nearly everyone was enthusiastic about the Lighted School House (a school kept open at night for a full range of adult education and community programs).

The idea for the school came from Katherine L. Allen, dean of Northeastern's Boston Bouve College of Physical and Recreation Education. The Boston Bouve College plan was a modification of the Flint, Michigan, Community School. Dean Allen developed the idea in June 1967, but the plan was a long time in coming to fruition. The original plan was to establish the school in Roxbury. Leaders in that black community were contacted during several months of discussion and formulation, but the community resisted the idea because there was no plan for a physical facility aside from classrooms. Unfortunately, a proposal for funding was sent to the Mott Fundation before the attitudes of the community were assessed. The Foundation made a site visit and learned of the community resistance; it did not fund the proposal.

Having failed in Roxbury, the idea was taken to the South End of Boston, a community of Greek, Arab, Puerto Rican, Chinese and black people (there are said to be 42 different ethnic groups living there). Planning meetings were held with the local community—one such meeting had 200 participants—and the proceedings were translated simultaneously into four different languages. As a result of these meetings, a proposal was written, and Asa Knowles, the president of the university, committed $25,000 from the university budget to start the program.

A full-time black director, William Brush, was hired, and courses for children and adults began. Classes for children ranged from kindergarten to eighth grade. Courses in basic reading and math were established, with a wide range of field trips to stimulate the children. They visited an astronomomical observatory, local university laboratories, and television stations and used the swimming pools and gyms of Boston Bouve College.

The major emphasis of the adult program was to provide English courses for Spanish-, Chinese-, and Greek-speaking adults. Initial enrollment was low, but Brush, the director, was not discouraged, because each week the number increased as the participants spread the word in the community.

The university gave full cooperation in providing materials and facilities for the school, and it explored various sources for funding and other assistance to expand the school's range of activities. Northeastern had no intention of expanding into or otherwise taking over the community. It simply wanted to provide whatever it could to an underprivileged community, with the hope of breaking down some of the barriers between town and gown.

At first hopes were high, but by the spring of 1970 a pall had fallen over the project, and everyone involved seemed disappointed and discouraged.

Several reasons are given for the schools's problems. One version put the responsibility on local leaders; another attributed the failure to leadership at Northeastern. The first version went this way, according to a university source:

Mr. Brush, the Director, did a good job getting the thing going. He would go from door to door explaining the idea, encouraging people to participate in the school. It was evident though from the beginning at the meetings that the community was suspicious of the establishment [Northeastern].

. . . the advisory board of the school was stacked with affluent people who didn't represent the people and were trying to wrest control of the school from the University. . . .

It all came to a head toward the first of the summer. Mr. Brush was offered a good job with the school he had left in New York City in order to come up here. We couldn't compete with their offer. . . . We didn't plan a summer program and resisted the advisory board's suggestion for one. They insisted on the program and made plans. Well, they sat-in on us; so we threw it into their laps. They hired a new director, a hard working, capable black woman, and they spent $10,500 of the $25,000 for the summer program. All during the summer there were fights about money.

We got a hard time all that summer. Toward fall, they came to us and asked us for another $25,000 for the second year. They wanted us to just give them the money. Well, we wanted more control than that, so we told them that we couldn't give them the money without administering the program. In the end we told them to raise the money themselves and administer the program themselves.

The other version attributed the failure to Northeastern's leadership:

> Boston Bouve just couldn't handle those people down in Castle Square. They couldn't handle the conflict stirred up by the Board. The Friends of Mackey School were suspicious of Northeastern. They wanted power to the people. Who are the people? In this case, the middle class or upwardly mobile working class. I guess it would have helped if Boston Bouve would have been represented by someone from a minority group.

Undoubtedly, elements of both stories are true. Community groups, in their new consciousness, can be demanding and difficult; and it takes special skill and a certain finesse to work with them. But democratic processes have never been easy, and perhaps a few hard knocks can be expected when universities take things to the people.

The Center for Continuing Education Much more effective than the Lighted School House and longer-lived than the Dropout School are the unique and varied activities of the Center for Continuing Education. The dean of this school is Israel Katz, known to all as Iz. He is a large, pleasant, outgoing man with the assurance and easy manner of one who knows his job well and is pleased with his achievements. Before coming to Northeastern, he was a professor of engineering at Cornell University and an engineering manager at General Electric.

Dean Katz's philosophy of continuing education is unusual: for him it is not adult education or extension work, but a unique provision of courses to upgrade or stretch the competencies of practitioners and professionals in nearly every field. Courses are generally presented in seminar or workshop format where the student becomes involved as a participant teacher. Resource people for these courses must be very adaptable to the needs of the group taking the course and steer away from an authoritarian attitude or lecture type of situation.

Courses provided by the center range from an Institute on Youth and Drugs for school counselors to an elaborate, semester-long series of courses on the state-of-the-art to help engineers and scientists stay abreast of technological advances both in their own fields and in peripheral areas. In the first, a group of counselors was brought to a large, elegant, old home (Henderson House) for an intensive 12-day course of study providing information about all aspects of drugs; they explored their own attitudes about drugs and drug abusers and visited Boston State Hospital's Addiction Unit and Odyssey House in New York City. The state-of-the-art series offered 67 different courses in engineering, ranging from statistics to laser light optics. These were held at a number of locations, including suburban schools.

The state-of-the-art courses best express Dean Katz's belief that education is a lifelong experience and that adult education should be a normal and necessary part of a person's working life. In this respect, Northeastern attempts to relate the latest developments in a profession or practice to the participant's knowledge and experience in his field of work.

The Youth and Drug Institute exemplifies the center's interest in attacking social and urban problems. Many such programs and courses are undertaken as a community service.

Courses at the center are grouped and developed under four different departments:

1 *Community services* range from institutes for construction workers designed to overcome racial prejudices to updating administrative skills for nursing home administrators.

2 *Continuing education in science and technology* is the largest of the four in terms of the number of students. It has a reputation for providing high-level courses.

3 *Continuing education in business* utilizes a broad range of techniques and subject matters, including T-groups and interpersonal relations groups, clinical psychology, and studies of autocratic and paternalistic behavior.

4 *Continuing education in professional science and engineering* generally acts as a direct consultant to engineering firms to determine the specific needs of a situation and as counsel in courses as needed. For example, at Raytheon, management had assumed that persons performing a specific job had working knowledge of applied trigonometry. This assumption was not borne out and was causing production problems. Raytheon contacted the Center for Continuing Education, which organized a workshop on trigonometry applied to crystal growth and fabrication.

Faculty for most center courses are recruited from among practitioners rather than from Northeastern itself; 80 percent come from business, industry, social agencies, or research institutions. These instructors work part time on a course-to-course basis. The center has been successful in getting very competent teachers and has a growing reputation in the Boston area for providing high-level training for graduate practitioners.

It has also been financially self-supporting. According to Dean Katz, the center showed a net income above a more than $1,000,000 budget for 1969, but after deducting the costs of low-income-community service courses this amounted to a break-even position. Despite this self-supporting performance, the program has met some resistance from regular university faculty. Dean Katz explained:

The faculty as a whole does not understand the Center and consequently is not in favor of what we are doing, but gradually we hope to win it over. It's a new step; we're doing difficult things and there are not many people who believe universities should be as aggressive as we are about going out to the local community and selling our courses. Someday the Center will be appropriately recognized at home.

This idea of expanding the concept of continuing education to reach persons already established in a job, practice, or profession is unusual. It seems to be in keeping with the rapid changes that are occurring in society and technology. Dean Katz summed up his position and the efforts of the center in this way:

With the seemingly steady increases in technology and the rapid social changes that are occurring today, individuals should be prepared to make several career changes over the course of their lifetime. Universities have to recognize this and make these changes possible for the individual. If we don't, we are going to have a country of bitter, discontented middle-age people who feel discarded by society. Our Center is meeting that problem, but other universities have to join in. Education is a lifelong process and universities should not be concerned only with the young or the middle classes.

The Black Students Program The special black students program was initiated at Northeastern in the fall of 1964, when 25 students were admitted with full scholarships for five years (in the co-op program) with funds provided by the Ford Foundation. These students were euphemistically called Ford scholars. One such scholar said of the group:

Yes, most of the group that I came in with have remained at the University and are doing well (12 of the original 25 graduated in June, 1969). But you wouldn't believe how the original 25 were selected. You have to give it to Whitey; he's always scheming. Nearly all of the original 25 were athletes, you know. The University used the 25 scholarships to strengthen their athletic teams. They used those scholarships to bring in more athletes.

Well, when we got organized, got ourselves together in 1966, this was the first issue we confronted the University on.

Each year 25 more black students were brought in under scholarships during 1965, 1966, and 1967. Beginning in 1965, a special summer preparatory program was initiated for black students, and this has been continued every year since.

After the death of Martin Luther King in the spring of 1968, black students of the Afro-American Association approached President Knowles and the university with 13 demands. One of these was an increase in the number of black freshmen to 50 for the fall of 1969. Dr. Knowles responded very positively to the students, as one black student relates:

Asa Knowles is a beautiful cat; he wants to cooperate. When we made our demands, he responded immediately and almost always in the affirmative. And what's more, he carried them out. Like we got more black students than we asked for last year. We asked for 50 and got 85.

Admission procedures for black students were streamlined: College Entrance Examination Board scores were not used, and students were accepted on the basis of their potential and motivation. If the student demonstrated a genuine concern to get in and succeed, he was accepted.

Financial aid is also generous. Martin Luther King Scholarships (of which there were 75 in the fall of 1969) provide full tuition, fees, books. and commuting expenses. If additional assistance is needed, it is given. As Roland Latham, the black assistant dean of students, says:

We try to meet all the needs of the students. If someone needs clothes, glasses, what have you, we come up with the money for them. We try to give them special housing consideration, try to get them housing close to the University. . . . Another policy we have—this one's brand-new—is the extended freshman year. If a student shows problems in adjustment and doesn't do as well as expected, we extend the freshman year. We let them do the freshman year in two years if they have to.

In general, relations between the university and the black student group (the Afro-American Association) are amicable. President Knowles anticipated some of the black students' demands before they were made.

In February 1969, black students proposed that the university establish an Afro-American institute and a Black Studies department. President Knowles agreed and encouraged the proposals. With little fanfare and few of the problems faced by other universities in the formation of similar programs, Northeastern provided a small building for the institute and staff to begin its operation.

Good relations between black students, the black community, and President Knowles are largely the result of efforts by Kenneth Williams, who was first an assistant to the president and later a coordinator of the Afro-American Institute. Williams is a young, dynamic, bearded, black man whose relations with both students and the president are excellent. With students he is casual and at ease; he can bang the table and rap with the best of them. With the president he is calm and articulate—a thoroughly reasonable man who resists the temptation to be co-opted by either side.

The Teacher Intern Program The Prototype Program for Teacher Education is attempting to bring Northeastern's College of Education together with two private ghetto schools (Roxbury Community School and the New School for Children) in a program to revise curriculum and training for teachers who plan to work in inner-city schools. According to William Quill, the program coordinator and assistant professor of education, traditional teacher training programs have done little to prepare teachers to work in such schools. His program will attempt to change teacher training by:

1 giving inner-city residents a significant role in the program—each of the three groups has equal voice in all decision making

2 allowing the interns, during their undergraduate education, to develop a curriculum that is appropriate and meaningful for children in inner-city schools

3 deemphasizing academic achievement for evaluating interns, and specifying the behavior skills and characteristics that make urban teachers effective

The program grew out of discussions among representatives of the Roxbury Community School and the New School for Children and Northeastern's associate dean of education, Ray Dethy, about the possibility of allowing uncertified teachers currently working in the community schools to attend Northeastern to obtain undergraduate degrees. The College of Education had no such program, but Dean Dethy proposed that the community schools and Northeastern get together to develop a prototype program that would allow interns to develop their own curriculum and course of study leading to a degree.

LEADERSHIP Most departments and schools of the university—many more than have been mentioned in this chapter—are involved with Boston and its problems. Their involvement is a result not only of the relationships between the community and Northeastern that arise out of the cooperative scheme of education, but also of the direction given to the university by its president, Asa Knowles.

Knowles is an unassuming, conservatively dressed, round-faced man, whose physical appearance belies his innovative ideas for Northeastern and its urban emphasis. Both students and faculty think that Knowles has been the force leading the university's attack on Boston's social problems. One faculty member summarized their attitude:

Old Ace [Asa] is really into things; he's tuned into urban problems and really responds. His door is open at any time to new ideas, and when he says he'll back you up, he does. He doesn't have any pretensions about Northeastern; he knows that it is a proletarian university and he wants to educate kids who really need it.

Dr. Knowles' leadership in dealing with urban problems has not been as easy or as popular as it has perhaps been made to sound here. Some at Northeastern resist his ideas and plans. The president tells his own story of this resistance:

Five years ago [in 1964], when I encouraged the University departments and staff to get involved with the city, the head of the Sociology Department said for all to hear, "Yes, if Dr. Knowles wants to get involved with the city, give him a broom and let him sweep Huntington Avenue (a particularly dirty street that borders the University)." So, you see, it has not always been a popular thing to do at Northeastern; but despite that, I have always felt that Northeastern should take the leadership in providing whatever services we could to the local community. Now the rest of the universities in Boston—Harvard, Boston University and Boston College—are getting on the bandwagon because they know that is where the money is.

8. Columbia: Turning the University Around

by Robert E. Price

In 1775, when Columbia University was still King's College of Wall Street, a mob of local townspeople marched on the campus seeking the neck of the college president, Miles Cooper, a known Tory sympathizer. While undergraduate Alexander Hamilton kept the angry crowd at bay, Cooper in his nightshirt scurried out the back window and down to the Hudson River. The next day he boarded ship for England, never to return. Columbia and its presidents have had problems with the city ever since.

Franklin Williams, when he assumed the post of director of Columbia's Urban Center, in 1968, described his task as no less than to "turn the University around." While able to halt to some degree the university's retreat, the Urban Center and the student revolt that occurred around the time it was started have hardly accomplished such wide-sweeping goals.

This chapter will first trace the history of Columbia's retreat from the city and its attempt to rebuild its neighborhood in its own image of a suitable academic environment. The major portion of the discussion will center on the formation and activities of the Urban–Minority Affairs Center as a result of a $10 million grant from the Ford Foundation in 1966.

RETREAT FROM THE CITY Columbia's institutional retreat from New York City began in 1857 when the college abandoned its buildings on the grounds of Trinity Episcopal Church and moved north to the site of what is now Rockefeller Center. The city soon caught up with the college, prompting another move uptown in 1897. The site chosen was a plateau in uptown Manhattan known as Morningside Heights. The "last escape" seemed to guarantee the college, now officially a university, an "academic" atmosphere. Columbia, "crowned and set upon a height," as the Alma Mater sings, was to become "the Acropolis of the Hudson."

Unfortunately, the Columbia trustees were not sufficiently far-sighted to purchase the entire Heights for university use. Faced with an almost unlimited amount of land available at nominal cost, they settled for a 16-square-block area. Still, in 1914 Columbia's historian Frederick Keppel could write: "One of our valued academic possessions is the fine view from the President's house over Morningside Park, across the city, and to the hills of Long Island." The advancing city soon spoiled the president's view. The residential neighborhood underwent a rapid process of urban evolution and decay. Other institutions began to move into the area. By 1947 the 14 institutions on the Heights found it necessary to form an organization, Morningside Heights, Incorporated (M.H., Inc.), to "promote the improvement of Morningside Heights as an attractive residential, educational, and cultural area." It employed a uniformed street patrol, largely financed by Columbia, and ran some small community service programs. The corporation also sponsored the construction of Morningside Gardens, a 1,000-unit middle-income housing development, and Grant Houses, a 2,000-unit low-income project, removing two blighted areas to the north of the Heights (Rauch, Feldman, & Leaderman, 1968).

As an educational institution Columbia was also undergoing change during this period. Before 1900 the student body was drawn largely from professional upper-middle-class, New York society. In the 1900s the college began to attract the intellectually ambitious and professionally oriented children of New York immigrants, particularly Jews. After World War II, however, the student body came to have a distinctly national character (Bell, 1966). The traditional, classical curriculum began to give way at Columbia as early as 1792, when professorships of economics, natural history, and French were established; but tradition died hard—Latin was maintained as an entrance requirement until 1916. The "irrelevance" of the classical curriculum in the mid-1900s almost deprived the college of students and revenue; a $140,000 gift from the state saved Columbia (Rudolph, 1965). A far greater threat to the college was the growing trend toward professionalism, which called into question the necessity for four-year institutions. Columbia survived the challenge, however, thanks to the concept of general education. The introduction of a general honors course on "great books" and a contemporary civilization course in 1917 represented Columbia's commitment to the concept that "there is a certain minimum of . . . [the Western] intellectual and spiritual tradition that a man must experience and understand if he is to be called educated." (Rudolph, 1965.) General education dominated the college without a break until 1954, when a majors system was introduced (Bell, 1966). The college was able to maintain its existence, despite its small size (2,700) in the midst of a large university (17,000) that annually awarded more Ph.D.'s than any other in the nation. Columbia College has remained an elite school, one in which 90 percent of the graduating class goes directly into professional or postgraduate education.

RENOVATING THE NEIGHBOR-HOOD The needs of a large university and the deterioration of the community led to conflict. The Faculty Civil Rights Group traced the history of the encounter in 1967. Columbia Provost Jacques Barzun described the neighborhood as "uninviting, abnormal, sinister, and dangerous." Of particular concern to the university was the existence of SROs: hotellike conversions of former apartment buildings, legally classified as single-room occupancies. The SROs had become principal housers of "deteriorated people," as Columbia planner Stanley Salmen called them. For example, the Bryn Mawr Hotel on 121st Street, when demolished in 1964, housed 90 relief clients, many of whom were alcoholics, addicts, and prostitutes, according to a study done by the Columbia School of Social Work.

Columbia proclaimed its intent to rid the neighborhood of a source of crime and restore it to its previous condition. Unable to flee the city any longer, the school decided to try to remake it in its own image. Salmen is quoted by the Faculty Civil Rights Group as saying: "We are looking for a community where the faculty can talk to people like themselves. We don't want a dirty group." Suggestions that Columbia might take the approach of instituting social service programs rather than removing SRO tenants were rejected. Since renewal of the neighborhood would primarily mean removing blacks, whose population had increased 700 percent from 1950 to 1960, and Puerto Ricans, whose numbers on the Heights had doubled, sensitive racial issues were involved.

Removal proceeded effectively: 6,700 of the 9,600 SRO tenants were removed between 1960 and 1968, reversing the population trends of the previous decade. Columbia described its success in "cleaning and restoring" the Heights:

Self-styled political leaders and other quarrelsome elements, often finding allies among professional politicians, have done much to impede the renewal plan. But Morningside Heights has been cleaned up anyway and is now one of the safer parts of the city. All but two SRO's have been eliminated and nobody really regrets their passing. (Faculty Civil Rights Group, 1967.)

What most upset the "self-styled political leaders" was Columbia's failure to abide by urban renewal guidelines. In response to a study sponsored by M.H., Inc., the city submitted to the federal government the Morningside Heights General Neighborhood Renewal Plan (GNRP), which was developed and revised over the years 1959 to 1964. Unhappy with the plan because it did not fulfill the university's desire to eliminate SROs and public housing between 110th Street and 123rd Street, Columbia accelerated its purchase of buildings before the GNRP could be approved. In January 1965, the GNRP was approved and a map issued supposedly showing the limits of institutional expansion. Within four months Columbia had purchased an SRO outside the limits set by the plan. As of September 1968, 58 of the 309 residential buildings in the neighborhood had been demolished, emptied, or converted for institutional use, and 20 of these were outside the limits shown on the map (Cox Commission, 1968).

Although nonprofit institutions were not required to provide any relocation services or grants to displaced tenants, Columbia, in January 1963, formed an Office of Neighborhood Services to "polish up its tarnished image," as its first director said. The tarnish was hardly removed by the university's actions to evict tenants who were reluctant to vacate. Holdouts were offered stipends in addition to regular relocation grants if they moved immediately. Rents were increased 25 percent in one SRO to "encourage the few people who were still there to leave," as Columbia phrased it. Occasionally building services and building security were allowed to deteriorate as an additional "inducement" to vacate. Extensive harassment took place at some dwellings, including surprise police raids and the plugging of keyholes while residents were away (Faculty Civil Rights Group, 1967; Rauch et al., 1968).

Columbia failed to correct these abuses, despite a penetrating report by the Faculty Civil Rights Group in December 1967. Thoroughly documenting Columbia's past policies, the group stated, "Institutional expansion combines the worst dangers of urban renewal with a complete absence of renewal's advantages and safeguards." The committee emphasized the need for an overall master plan for institutional expansion and made four recommendations:

1   Efforts should be instituted to revive an economically and ethnically integrated and balanced community on Morningside Heights.

2   Housing planning should incorporate the idea of mixed community-faculty-student dwellings.

3   Community service programs should be initiated by the university.

4   Community representatives should be involved in the planning and operating stages of the above.

The Gym   The resentment the community felt toward Columbia's expansion policies became focused on one issue: the gym. For two decades Columbia had contemplated building a new gymnasium to replace its antiquated, cramped facility located underneath the Uris Hall Business School. In 1959 definite plans were drafted. An $11.6 million Columbia–community gym was to be erected on a steep, rocky slope at the south end of Morningside Park. The gym would occupy 2.1 acres of the 30-acre park that separates the Heights from Harlem. The Columbia facility was anticipated to cost $10 million, the separate community portion $1.6 million. Columbia was to construct the community gym, pay for all athletic equipment, and pay for staff supervision of the community gym. The university's estimate of annual heating costs alone for the community facility was $75,000. The gym would be open all year without fee.

On the whole the plan met with enthusiastic endorsement. The city had in recent years poured $500,000 into Morningside Park, which it had first taken over in 1870. Despite this, the park was still labeled by police as a "very to extremely hazardous" area and an area of "light public use." The park was rarely used by persons in the community, and it was almost never used at night. It was a notorious hangout for muggers, and one of the world's largest narcotics traffic centers was located on its fringes. One of the few distinguishing monuments in the Park is Edgar Walton's Bear and Fawn Fountain, but no one can ever remember seeing water in it. The only area of real use in the park was the Columbia–community playground at the south end of the park, opened in 1957 after Columbia spent $250,000 to reclaim the land, construct a playing field, and build a small field house. Some 2,500 teen-agers in orga-

nized teams took part in baseball, touch football, and track programs run by Columbia. The playground was constructed by
Columbia for the community and leased back to Columbia for
university use during the academic year.

Many community leaders heralded Columbia's gymnasium plan
as a landmark in university-community cooperation. Little or no
opposition was voiced as the plan cleared necessary approval from
the mayor, the board of estimate, the city council, the municipal
arts commission, two successive parks commissioners, both houses
of the state legislature, and the governor. In order to lease park land
to Columbia, the city had to go through the legislature. In 1959
enabling legislation was passed, and it was signed into law by
Governor Nelson Rockefeller in April 1960. The lease, which called
for Columbia to pay $3,000 a year rent, was approved by the board
of estimate after a public hearing in July 1961. In August 1961
Columbia signed a 100-year lease with the city.

Because of a shortage of funds, Columbia was unable to begin
immediate construction of the gym. In fact, the deadline for groundbreaking—in order for the lease to remain valid—was postponed
several times. During the delay opposition began to develop. Two
new parks commissioners under Mayor John Lindsay opposed the
plan; they felt the community was getting too little out of the deal.
The mood and level of political sophistication in the Harlem community were also undergoing change during this period. Columbia's
administration was insensitive to this. As the student documenters
of the student revolt phrased it, "The gym . . . was in the best tradition of white liberal aid to the disadvantaged. . . . The Columbia
administration and Trustees could not understand that now paternalistic liberalism was no longer wanted" (Avorn, 1969). In response to community pressure, Columbia altered its plans and in
October 1967 announced that it was adding a community swimming pool to the facility, raising the community portion of the gym
from 12.5 percent to 15 percent. Opponents still demonstrated
against "gym crow" even after groundbreaking began. H. Rap
Brown appeared before a community group and told them that if
the gym were constructed, they should "blow it up . . . burn it
down." Columbia took the position that "construction of the gym is
now a *fait accompli.*"

And so it appeared until the student demonstration of April 1968.
The first student demand acceded to by the university was a sus-
pension of construction on the gym. After a year of consultation

with the community, which revealed majority support for the gym but enough opposition to create serious problems, the trustees abandoned plans for the gym in the park (Nash & Epstein, 1968). Columbia claimed to have lost $5 million—the cost of terminating construction after contracts had been signed. In addition, much haggling with the city followed about who would pay for rehabilitation of the construction site, which remained a gaping hole.

A DECLINING UNIVERSITY Gaping holes were in evidence at numerous other facets of Columbia's life. Christopher Jencks and David Riesman described Columbia in not too complimentary terms in *The Academic Revolution:* "Its leadership is bankrupt, its location dysfunctional, and its faculty deteriorating." The leadership problem was one of both structure and personality. During the 42-year tenure of President Nicholas Murray Butler (1902–1945), Columbia's administration was centralized in the hands of one man—Butler. His charismatic leadership single-handedly built Columbia into a great university—but at great expense, for no alumni fund-raising mechanisms and no cohesive university structure were created. During Butler's declining years and during the weak presidencies of Dwight Eisenhower and Grayson Kirk, the university moved to a decentralized structure. Each university division became a fiefdom, with its own fund-raising program. This led to the enrichment of schools with strong alumni loyalty and the impoverishment of others. The Cox Commission report compared the "new and well-equipped professional school buildings with the old and inadequate structures that house the College and Graduate Facilities" (Cox Commission, 1968, p. 33).

Leadership problems pervaded the institution. The style of Columbia's planner Stanley Salmen, who often was the university's representative to the community, has been illustrated previously. Provost Jacques Barzun and Vice-Provost Herbert Deane often expressed themselves in ways most likely to alienate the community and students. Kirk was a weak leader. A student slogan ran: "Butler reigned and ruled. Ike reigned but did not rule. Kirk neither reigns nor rules."

If the administration was isolated from the educational situation and the community, the 24 trustees were even more so. That self-perpetuating body was composed of a homogeneous elite of banking executives, real estate brokers, communications and mass media leaders, and utilities executives. No scholars, no artists, no blacks, no women, no labor leaders, no former public servants were on the board. The trustees' average age was over sixty (*Who Rules Columbia?* 1968).

Columbia's academic standing had begun to drop. Faculty salaries, according to the AAUP ratings, had dropped in national ranking during the period from 1963–64 to 1967–68 from fifth to ninth to fifteenth to twelfth to seventeenth. A 1966 study by the American Council on Education showed that Columbia's graduate programs, which in 1957 were among the top three in the nation, ranked consistently below fifth. In April 1967, the Ford Foundation omitted Columbia from the 10 universities to which it granted $41.5 million for restructuring doctoral programs, stating that Columbia "lacked motivation for reform" (Cox Commission, 1968).

Some changes had been begun at Columbia. The middle administrative level was particularly weak because Columbia had but 1 vice-president and 31 deans. In 1967 a major administrative shake-up removed Barzun from the position of provost and replaced him with David Truman, a man of similarly solid academic credentials who, as dean of the college, had maintained excellent rapport with students and alumni. A number of vice-presidents were named to bolster the middle administrative evel. Many felt that Truman was being groomed for the presidency.

The administrative shake-up did not prevent new problems, such as the Strickman affair. Robert Strickman, a free-lance chemist, claimed to have perfected a cigarette filter far superior to any other on the market. Partly to benefit the university and mostly to establish credibility for his invention, he agreed to turn over all rights to it to Columbia. Columbia enthusiastically accepted and announced the agreement with great fanfare in July 1967. This was a questionable move, coming at a time when the United States Surgeon General was engaged in a massive campaign against cigarette smoking as a health hazard. But even worse was the fact that Columbia had not even tested the filter. Later tests revealed the filter to be of limited worth. Columbia eventually surrendered its interest, and the trustees issued the following meek statement: "The University feels that it owes it to the public to state candidly that it made a well-intentioned mistake in entering a highly controversial and competitive commercial field." (Ridgeway, 1968.)

As provost, Truman became the spokesman for the university and thus was identified with Kirk in the students' revolt of 1968.

He followed Kirk in departure from Columbia after the crisis—Kirk to retirement, Truman to the presidency of Mt. Holyoke College. A renowned diplomat, Andrew Cordier became Columbia's acting president and later, when several candidates—Martin Meyerson, John Gardner, and Alexander Heard, among them—refused the job, president. Eventually, William McGill, chancellor of the University of California, San Diego, was named president.

THE FORD FOUNDATION GRANT

In 1961 Columbia University rejected the idea of a centralized fund-raising campaign; five years later, on November 1, 1966, it embarked on the largest fund drive ever announced by a university—a $200 million, three-year effort. Kicking off the drive was a $35 million grant from the Ford Foundation, the largest single-institution grant ever made by that organization. The grant was in two parts: $25 million was on a four-to-one matching basis; the remaining $10 million was designated for the "establishment of a broad new program in urban and minority affairs."

In announcing the grant, Ford President McGeorge Bundy indicated the $10 million could be used for projects ranging from "special research appointments" to "experimental action in ghetto communities." The grant was apparently unexpected and unsolicited by the university. There seemed to be confusion from the outset on how the money should be spent. Kirk maintained that the program would be "likely to make a greater contribution in terms of research and training than in terms of direct action." Champion Ward, vice-president of the Ford Foundation, emphasized both "action projects in the surrounding community" and work within the university for "improved understanding and training" in the field of urban-minority problems. While Columbia announced no plans for the inclusion of community leaders in discussions, Ford indicated that such community participation was expected. But, Ward said, "we feel this is something for Columbia's initiative." While Kirk said that a major role of the money would be the coordination of current university programs in urban affairs, Ward stressed the establishment of new activities rather than "merely the traditional notion of doing a good job of what you are already doing."

The Advisory Committee and Council

Columbia's first step after accepting the grant was to appoint a 5-man advisory committee and a 24-man advisory council. All the members were from the university; except for two student members of the council, all were professors. No community representatives and no minority representatives were named. Heading the committee was General Studies Dean Clarence Walton, later named interim director of the Center for Urban-Minority Affairs.

The committee commissioned two studies: an inventory of Columbia's existing activities in the area (Caplow, 1966), and a study of programs at Harvard, Yale, Chicago, Penn, and Michigan (Nash & Nash, 1968). The Columbia survey reported: "Columbia College, General Studies, and the Graduate Faculties are probably unique among comparable components of major universities in the almost total omission of urban and minority issues from their curricula." Only one course in each of the undergraduate divisions was considered relevant to the area. The survey concluded: "It follows that any serious increase of instructional offerings related to urban and minority problems would require the recruitment of new faculty members with appropriate qualifications and interests."

Some of the professional schools, particularly Social Work and Public Health, were given much better ratings. Others, like the Law School, which only in 1967 introduced a course called "The Law and the Poor," fared nearly as badly as the undergraduate schools (Caplow, 1966).

Student field work was another area inventoried. Only at the School of Social Work was course credit given for student work in the community. That this had not received much thought at Columbia did not surprise anyone who had read Daniel Bell's book, *The Reforming of General Education,* a year-long effort funded by the Carnegie Corporation, to study the Columbia curriculum and suggest changes. Only one paragraph in the 300-plus pages of the book is devoted to "action programs" or "work programs" as a part of the educational experience of students.

The Columbia College Citizenship Council program (Cit Council) was singled out as one of the most meaningful involvements of the university in the community. Founded in 1957, the program soon became one of the largest college student volunteer programs in the country. In 1965–66, it had 1,100 volunteers; in 1966–67 the number increased to 1,600.

In the late 1960s the Cit Council reflected the changing mood of the student population at Columbia. The council began to get more involved in radical politics, and the number of volunteers dropped to 550 in 1968–69. When Columbia students called a strike in the spring of 1967, the governing board of Cit Council voted not to take a stand on this political issue. A minority of the board, however, offered the council offices to the SDS-led strike committee as an information headquarters. This polarized the council and led the "liberals," who felt that students could still provide meaningful service to ghetto communities, to "dissolve" the Cit Council in December 1968 and establish themselves as the Columbia-Barnard Community Service Council. They took with them 400 of the 550 volunteers and the program's paid director, Roderick Derkin. The "radicals," who felt "political" issues to be the order of the day, eventually came to an agreement with the liberals on division of facilities and budget, and both programs continued in operation.

In addition to curriculum and student field work, the Columbia survey looked at basic research, which was defined broadly as "any inquiry designed to contribute to public knowledge about urban and minority problems or to uncover general principles useful in solving them." The study concluded: "Even by this flexible criterion, there is little to be counted at Columbia at present." The Columbia Council for Research in the Social Sciences, whose grants support the personal, long-term research interests of the faculty, approved 24 projects for 1966–67, only 1 having anything to do with New York or local minorities. In the area of applied research, the university came out somewhat better. The Schools of Social Work, Law, and Architecture and the Bureau of Applied Social Research led the way (Caplow, 1966).

The Advisory Committee Report

Following these initial studies, the advisory committee drew up a report, which was completed in mid-June 1967. In preparing the report, the committee claimed to have consulted many university departments, several governmental officials, and over 200 representatives of the Harlem community. However, only a month before the report was completed, the three student members of the advisory council resigned, denouncing the council as "a sham." The committee had had only three meetings in five months, took no votes, reached no decisions, and had drawn up the report keeping no minutes of its meetings that could be presented to the whole council. Nonetheless, in October 1967, the first phase of Columbia's Urban-Minority Affairs program was announced, using up $2.7 million of the Ford grant.

The report introduced to the public three pilot programs that had received advance approval and were already in operation, supported by an allocation of $180,170. One was a program conducted by the

School of Social Work and the St. Luke's Hospital Community Psychiatry Division to provide the first Columbia-supported social service program for residents of single-room occupancy buildings. A second pilot program involved 35 Columbia law students in work with specific legal problems of Harlem poor people. The third was a grant to the 10-year-old Law School program for Effective Justice to study protection of the poor against malpractices in the collection of small debts and the eviction of tenants.

In addition to the three pilot programs, the report announced several new projects. The largest single program grant was $600,000 to Teachers College to improve Harlem schools and to develop educational leadership in the community. Professor Francis Ianni was placed in charge, and the exact specifications of the program were not outlined. Teachers College officials admitted that an allocation of such a sum without specific project plans was "unusual." The committee had originally recommended a $350,000 program to transform one existing Harlem school into a community school directly operated by Columbia and the Harlem community. The multiple-approach program, as opposed to this single-school approach, was expected to involve 50 students from Teachers College with 10 different school-community groups. The work of the East Harlem Community Resource Center, a clearinghouse for community educational groups, was also to be expanded.

Another major beneficiary of Ford's largess was the Institute of Urban Environment of the School of Architecture, which received $179,000 for a detailed analysis of Harlem housing needs.

Another $430,000 went to five new community involvement projects:

1 Creation of an Industrial and Commercial Development Association, involving Harlem business leaders, the Interracial Council for Business Opportunity, and faculty from the Graduate School of Business and the Department of Economics

2 Creation of a Development Division to seek out, enroll, and give special professional and technical job training to minority adults who did not meet Columbia's admission standards

3 Efforts by a group of doctors from Harlem Hospital to train community people to be medical laboratory assistants, labor and delivery room technicians, and technical nursing assistants

4 Efforts to enlarge cooperation between the School of the Arts and various cultural groups in Harlem

5   Emergency action to save 5,000 items in the Schomberg Collection of Negro history, literature, and art, which were in danger of physical deterioration.

THE CENTER FOR URBAN-MINORITY AFFAIRS   The principal recommendation of the committee report was that a Center for Urban-Minority Affairs be created to coordinate and evaluate all these programs. It was established with an initial allocation of $111,500 and a $500,000 fund to provide doctoral fellowships in Negro history and urban problems. Further, a $250,000 endowment was set up to ensure a place for the center in the university after the Ford money was exhausted. A director was to be appointed to report directly to the president. The committee recommended that he be given professional rank with tenure. Two associate directors were to be named: one for community programs and one for urban-minority studies. The former post was to be "significantly different from traditional University assignments" and was to be filled by someone who knew Harlem through previous work with the community in nonacademic ways. The latter was to be a man of "scholarly attainments" (*Report of the President's Committee,* 1967).

Columbia's search for personnel to fill these positions revealed some significant modifications of the recommendations. The staff, and ultimately the Urban Center office itself, took on a distinctly Peace Corps flavor. The director appointed on March 7, 1968, was Franklin Williams, former regional administrator for Africa of the Peace Corps and, at the time of his appointment, United States ambassador to Ghana. Williams hardly seemed to fit the criteria suggested by the advisory committee. He was not a Ph.D. and did not, therefore, receive a faculty appointment, much less tenure. Although black and a native New Yorker, his experience for the preceding five years had been in Africa. He was addressed by some of his colleagues as "Ambassador." "Frank is just out of touch with the ghetto," one critic commented. In December 1968, Roger Kuhn, formerly Williams's deputy in the Peace Corps administration in Africa, was named deputy director of the center. At the time of his appointment, he was a professor of law at George Washington University, specializing in poverty law. Ewart Guinier, a veteran of community involvement in the Jamaica section of Queens, was named associate director. Significantly, Guinier's post was made inferior to Kuhn's, despite the recommendation by the committee that they be equivalent.

In a November press conference Williams made it clear that the

Ford grant was not designed to make Columbia an administrator of "an antipoverty program in Harlem." He reported having found in the community "suspicion as to who I am and why I am here" and "an impression that Columbia bought themselves a colored boy to solve problems. They will be sadly mistaken," he said. He then proceeded to outline a role for the Urban Center as a "catalyst for change." Community programs were to be funded when they were community-initiated and involved Columbia faculty, students, or facilities. Columbia would use the Ford funds as "seed money." The center divided its activities into four areas:

1 Curriculum development

2 Minority recruitment and funding

3 Research

4 Community programs

In each area, limited successes were achieved and problems developed.

Curriculum Development A year after the initial allocation for action projects, Ford granted $1.8 million to endow three chairs in the graduate faculties in the fields of urban economics, sociology, and history and government. Some questions were raised as to the appropriateness of this use of money designated for "urban-minority" affairs. Community leaders felt the money should have gone for community projects. Some in the university felt that, in addition to setting up chairs, money should have been set aside to provide these new professors with research staffs so that they might make a greater impact on the university.

These questions, however important, are secondary to the mystery of why Columbia took so long to find persons to fill the chairs. Only one of the three chairs was filled by September 1969, nearly three years after the funds were granted. Charles Hamilton, co-author with Stokely Carmichael of the book *Black Power,* assumed a professorship in the government department. Internal faculty politics delayed the other appointments.

Perhaps the most ambitious project of the Urban Center was the 1968–69 Curriculum Project, a complete report on curriculum, current and planned, dealing with urban and minority affairs, with recommendations for additions and improvement. Joseph Colmen, former director of research for the Peace Corps, was hired to direct the study. The study accumulated several volumes of material. A survey of students was conducted by the Bureau of Applied Social Research; the community was surveyed by a Harlem-based body, the Community Educational Associates. The report, entitled *The Human Uses of the University,* was submitted to the university in November 1969. Its recommendations were sweeping. It called for the establishment of a School of National Studies to coordinate a comprehensive degree program in urban studies and ethnic studies and to administer a wide range of community service projects.

The report stated that a school was desirable because it would have its own budget, its own faculty and faculty loyalty, and its own degrees. It would be easier under that structure to cross disciplinary lines and to avoid duplication. The school would have departments of ethnic studies and urban studies. The ethnic studies department would provide:

1 an undergraduate major in Afro-American studies

2 an undergraduate survey course in Afro-American studies for nonmajors

3 undergraduate courses in Puerto Rican studies

4 a graduate program in Afro-American studies

5 a department of American intercultural studies, presenting an interdisciplinary approach to issues of ethnicity and race relations

6 a student cultural center

The urban studies department would carry on the same kind of program with field work integrated into the curriculum. Also suggested was a Collegium of the City, a one-year experimental college program for selected students in the two departments of the school.

To coordinate the programs of the school with the community, an Ethnic and Urban Research, Information, and Community Center would be set up to provide consultation services to community programs and to mediate conflicts. To coordinate the programs of the school with those of other university divisions, the report recommended a university-wide Council on Urban and Ethnic Affairs (*The Human Uses,* 1969).

The Curriculum Project report met immediate resistance. Columbia's black student organizations criticized it for treating "the cultural and physical survival of black people as a mere abstract and theoretical issue." The student newspaper, however, offered its endorsement. The administration response was less enthusiastic. President Cordier estimated that instructional salaries alone for the school would amount to $1.5 million per year. The vice-president for administration, Warren Goodell, said this would mean some other division of the university would have to be eliminated. Provost Peter Kenen said, "The School would cost more money than we have for the whole University program. . . . I don't think you'll see the School for National Affairs here." Because the project was too ambitious and had no solid support, it became just one more divisive factor.

Some positive steps were taken in the curriculum area, despite the lack of action on these major recommendations. In March 1969, Columbia College offered its first black history class. That development was not without problems: the black students walked out on the white instructor early in the term. Money from the Urban Center brought in black guest lecturers and saved the course, although the white instructor continued to be in charge through 1969–70. The School of General Studies started an interdisciplinary major in urban studies in 1968–69, and Barnard began a similar program involving 30 students in 1969–70.

The two divisions of the university that were most progressive in adopting curricular programs relevant to urban problems were the School of Architecture and the School of Social Work. Architecture's most outstanding program was the East Harlem Urban Planning Studio, later the Community Development and Planning Studio (Kolodny, 1969). Formed in the spring of 1968 in cooperation with the Real Great Society, an indigenous youth movement working primarily with educational programs, this program provided a way for students, principally those in the Urban Planning Division of the school, to be involved in actual planning activities rather than classroom simulated projects, which successfully simulate physical design problems but often miss political, economic, and social factors.

Among the projects students undertook for course credit were:

1 planning and designing a storefront community center

2 planning a real estate management and maintenance training institute for East Harlem

3 establishing a six-week course in cost estimating for 33 members of a Harlem-based professional association of minority contractors

4 designing an intra-area transit system for East Harlem, consisting of two jitney-bus loops, that was to be owned and operated by the community

5 publishing a procedural handbook on the use of vacant buildings, storefronts, and lots by community groups

6 designing a plaza and festival center in an East Harlem marketing area

7 assisting in the establishment of a community center to train residents for jobs in the printing trades

By February 1969 one-quarter of the students in the school were working with community groups.

The School of Social Work, founded in 1904 and affiliated with Columbia since 1940, has been by nature involved in urban minority affairs. As Dean Samuel Finestone remarked, "There is not a single class we give which is not related to the urban crisis. That's what our profession is about when we are in the city." The school has been one of the leaders in shifting the focus of social work training from the caseworker approach to the community organization approach.

Mobilization for Youth, the real father of the antipoverty program, began at Columbia. A 1968 student strike led to even more rapid movement, as students gained almost equal representation on curriculum committees of the School of Social Work. One of the results of increased student involvement has been the broadening of field placement. Students doing community organizing were placed in two nontraditional organizations: Local 1199 of the Drug and Hospital Workers Union and the national office of CORE. With grants from the Urban Center and the Carnegie Corporation, a Leadership Cadre program was begun in 1968, providing scholarships and stipends for three blacks and three Puerto Ricans recommended by community organizations to undertake a two-year program in community organizing, leading to an M.S.W. (Berengarten, 1969).

Other divisions of the university, such as the Law School and Teachers College, began to make progress in these areas, although they did not become nearly as deeply involved as the Schools of Social Work and Architecture.

Minority Recruitment and Funding In December 1969 the Urban Center, under the leadership of Richard Thornell, issued a report on its work in support of increased minority student enrollment (*Toward Equal Opportunity*, 1969).

It painted a picture of uneven progress. Throughout the university, minority enrollment had increased from 4.9 percent to 6.8 percent. In several divisions of the university, little progress had been made. The Engineering School showed an increase of only 2 students out of 700. There were no minority students at all in the School of Dentistry; only 3 of 250 Nursing School students were from minority groups. The College of Physicians and Surgeons accepted only 4 of 40 black applicants in its class of 132, leaving its percentage of minority students at 1.8. The School of General Studies, theoretically the division that should have been most open to minority students, enrolled only 2.7 percent of its degree candidates from minorities. Dean John Bourne explained that the almost total absence of scholarship funds was a major barrier to any serious effort by General Studies to expand minority enrollment.

Three of the most progressive units of the university were the Schools of Social Work, Architecture, and Journalism. At the School of Social Work, a student strike in the spring of 1970 brought about an administrative commitment to a program of recruiting and financial aid that would raise the percentage of minority students from 10 to 33. The School of Architecture in one year raised its minority enrollment from 2.9 percent to 10.4 percent. Urban Center funding for recruiting was a contributory factor.

The Journalism School, in addition to raising its percentage of regular degree-program minority students from 8.8 to 18.6, conducted a special summer program for minority students that met with great success. In response to the Kerner Commission report, which criticized the mass media for their lack of minority employees, the school set up a program in the summer of 1968 under the direction of Fred Friendly, former news director of CBS. Students were given tuition exemption and living stipends or family allowances. The eight-week program trained 20 men and women. In 1969, a ten-week program took 36 persons (out of 125 applicants) — 31 black, 4 Puerto Rican, and 1 Mexican-American. Most of the students had been involved in communications, but a number had had no previous experience. They spent half the course time in class and half covering stories. All the graduates found jobs in communications.

Most of the public focus in the area of minority enrollment was on Columbia College. The Student Afro-American Society (SAS) began to demonstrate and work actively in this area after its abortive cooperation with SDS in the student strike of 1968 (Avorn, 1969). In April 1969, the college allocated $2,500 to cover the expenses of black students on recruiting trips. Progress in the college was slow at first. The number of minority students in the roughly 700-man freshman class was only 7 in 1964; it increased to 17 in 1965 and to 31 in 1966. In 1967 and 1968, the admissions office accepted roughly half the black applicants, as opposed to a third of all applicants. Still, the number of minority freshmen was only 29 in 1968, about 4 percent. The SAS criticized the administration for racist admissions and financial aid policies. The administration responded that 95 percent of black students were on scholarship as compared to 44 percent overall.

The college has continued to make progress, however, and its projections for 1970–71 showed that almost 25 percent of its entering class would be minority, a dramatic two-year increase. The graduate faculties, which had only 1.9 percent minority enrollment in 1969, also anticipated great improvement.

The recruiting picture for minority faculty members was less promising than that for students. The Urban Center made a systematic effort, under the direction of black theater historian Anne Reid, to locate black Ph.D.'s and refer them to various departments of the university. She met with deans and department heads to ascertain their needs. Then she tracked down blacks who had doctorates from the institutions from which Columbia usually drew faculty members, and asked if they were interested in teaching at Columbia. The first year's efforts resulted in about 50 referrals, but internal departmental considerations resulted in few appointments. Two divisions of the university, the Schools of Law and Business, gave up their efforts at recruitment. Dean William Fry of the Law School said that any black lawyer qualified for the school's faculty could make 50 percent more money in his law practice than Columbia could offer and be more in the forefront of social change than he could in a faculty position.

Research A wide variety of small research programs were supported by the Urban Center. Among the more prominent were research on the impact of law on blacks, conducted by Urban Center Fellow Robert Carter, former general counsel of the NAACP, and research on public welfare policy, conducted by Professors Richard Cloward and Frances Piven of the School of Social Work. Only 5 percent of the

Urban Center grants went to research, during a period in which $6.6 million of the $10 million Ford grant was used (Urban Center, 1969).

Community Programs The Urban Center has been involved, directly or indirectly, in a large number of community projects, in fields ranging from extension education and job training to labor relations, management consultation, film making, and development of television programs.

The Development Division
One of the major recommendations of the original advisory committee on the Urban Center was that a Development Division be set up under the auspices of the School of General Studies (Report of the President's Committee, 1967). General Studies had become a school in 1947, replacing the Extension Division of the university. The Development Division would, in effect, reactivate the extension concept, which had been lost as General Studies became less of an adult education division and more of an elite undergraduate college, primarily for those who had begun college elsewhere. The Development Division began operation in the summer of 1968 with a program for East Harlem residents in English as a second language. The project soon expanded to train a group of antipoverty workers in interview methods, report writing, and record keeping. In the first nine months of operation, 250 adults took part in Development Division programs.

Indirectly associated with the Development Division has been a program for upgrading minority employees. Columbia's history of employment practices has not been a very proud one. Eruptions of dissatisfied workers occurred as early as 1936. A student report by the Citizenship Council in the spring of 1968 documented Columbia's struggle against efforts to unionize nonacademic employees (Isaacson, Chrenstein, Rosen, Savage, & Waldman, 1968). The Transport Workers' Union represented service and maintenance personnel for many years, but efforts by CORE, SDS, and Local 1199 of the Drug and Hospital Workers Union to organize food service employees and other nonacademic workers met with staff resistance. (The administration is so defensive about this history that Business Manager Joseph Nye would not grant the author an interview, but required that all questions be submitted in writing.) The labor situation was finally resolved when, in April 1969, the New

York state legislature repealed a statute allowing nonprofit institutions to deny their employees the right to unionize.

Wages at Columbia were quite low and, as a result turnover was high. The controller's office, one of the poorest-paying, had almost a 50 percent annual turnover rate. According to the personnel office, Columbia's salaries at the entry level are comparable with those offered elsewhere in the city, but at the administrative assistant–executive secretary level the university cannot compete. Columbia estimates that about half of its employees from the maintenance level through the administrative assistant level are minority persons.

The advisory committee to the Urban Center, in its original report, recommended that, independent of Ford funds, the university and other Morningside Heights institutions undertake a program to become model employers. Among the recommended steps were more realistic criteria for employment, improved methods of job training, special remedial courses, in-service courses to develop and upgrade skills, improved promotional ladders, and establishment of employment-related services, such as day-care facilities for the children of working mothers (Report of the President's Committee, 1967).

Faced with a serious shortage of trained workers and the recommendations of the committee, Columbia hired Warren Kynard, a former Army personnel administrator, to develop an educational uplift program. Columbia thus committed itself to the approach of hiring entry-level people and then upgrading their skills. The program was open to all employees, but special priority was given to members of minority groups. No academic requirements were set. Many classes were scheduled during working hours to maximize employee incentive.

By the summer of 1969, 300 persons had graduated from the program; by August 1970 the number had risen to 663. The majority of the students took "English as a Second Language," but courses were also offered in accounting, business English, key punch operation, general mathematics, reading comprehension, stenography, and typing. No guarantee of promotion was offered on completion; promotion was left to the employing department. In addition, Kynard set up a Vestibule Clerical School, taking 10 minority women recruited from the State University Urban Center in Manhattan. They attended six weeks of all-day classes, were paid a minimum wage while doing so, and were guaranteed a job upon completion. All graduated and were employed by Columbia. After a year, 9 of the 10 were still working. Kynard also set up a workshop for supervisory personnel to sensitize them to the problems of minority employees.

Similar upgrading programs were offered in other university divisions. At the Computer Center the individual efforts of an administrative assistant, Sheila Creith, led to Step Forward, a 19-week program in office skills. She recruited nine other Columbia employees to do the teaching, lobbied with deans and department chairmen for space and equipment, and recruited 37 students for the program through 30 community agencies and 50 churches.

In sum, a number of meaningful steps were taken in what had been one of Columbia's weak points. As late as the spring of 1970, however, Columbia was still receiving complaints about discrimination in its food service facilities. At the same time, a group called the Day Care Action Coalition was putting pressure on the university to provide space for free day care for 300 children of Columbia faculty, staff, and students.

MBA management consultants

The Business School appointed Hughie Mills to the position of assistant dean for community relations, and the Urban Center paid his salary. Among the first things Mills did, in 1968, was to set up the MBA Management Consultant program to assist black entrepreneurs in Harlem. The program was developed in response to a request from Harlem businessmen, who now compose its board of directors. Teams of two or three students and a faculty supervisor provided counseling. For example, the first client was Andrew Gainer of the New York Gas and Maintenance Company. His small firm was bogged down because it had no formal accounting system, and Gainer had to be personally involved in all its operations. Counseling helped get the business systematized, and Gainer became the first vice-president of the consultant program's board of directors. Another client, who owned a grocery store, received help in applying for a modernization loan from the Small Business Administration, which led his sales to double.

The program did not start as a learning experience, but became for many of the traditionally conservative Business School students their first actual contact with minority persons. It involved 100 students, many working as much as 20 hours a week, although maximum payment was $3 an hour for six hours. No course credit was given.

University purchasing office

Another effort in this area was the opening of a university purchasing office in Harlem in 1968. Purchasing representative Junius Robinson tried to stimulate university buying from Harlem businessmen, fewer than 10 of whom were then selling to Columbia. Business Manager Nye said that the office would attempt to "guide the Harlem businessman through the many channels necessary to deal with as large an institution as this University." Hughie Mills reported that the office had some success in such buying areas as detergents, furniture, and printing. "It has had a healthy psychological impact on racist attitudes here," he added.

The School of the Arts

The School of the Arts and the School of General Studies are the most impoverished divisions of the university. Both also have considerable direct contact with the community. The School of the Arts has become substantially involved in community affairs, because the Urban Center has financed a liaison person to the community, Barbara Barnes. The center provided both funds and initiative because pressure did not come from students or faculty here as it did in many schools. Three projects in particular are worthy of mention.

1   A combined graduate seminar in black culture and creative writing workshop was set up under the direction of black author John Killens. The Urban Center paid his salary. Killens selected 15 community people and 5 graduate students to participate in the workshop.

2   Twelve technicians from three Harlem theaters took part in a Theater Technical Training program, spending 4 hours a week in courses on basic carpentry, lighting, and painting, and 20 hours divided between projects at their own theaters and projects at Columbia. The Urban Center provided six stipends, instructors' salaries, and materials.

3   The Urban Center provided money for the creation of a Community Film Board in January 1969. Before this, the center had funded the making of *Second Chance* (a film on the Phoenix House drug treatment program), a film on the teaching of black culture in the public schools, and three films entitled *Black Politics in Newark, The Poor People's Campaign,* and *Black Students in the Columbia Disturbance of 1968.* The program forced a real confrontation with the School of the Arts, and the Community Film Board

was set up to process all future requests for funds by black film makers. The board had hoped to establish a processing lab, which would have provided a new industry in the community as well as a new course for students. This would have cut the cost of film making, but the $92,000 that was needed was not forthcoming.

Barbara Barnes feels that these programs have had little impact on the School of the Arts: "My position has no leverage; my only weapon is moral suasion. Since no money from the School has been involved, it has made no real sacrifice and thus evidenced no real commitment."

East Harlem Community Resource Center
The Urban Center has provided assistance to the East Harlem Community Resource Center, established jointly by Teachers College and the community in January 1967. The center is a clearinghouse for community educational services, staffed by two members of the Horace Mann–Lincoln Institute, which is headed by Francis Ianni. The center has been involved in tutoring programs, a drama workshop, and a community newspaper. A group of high school students were supervised in a study of housing that received much attention from political leaders. The center also ran a World of Testing program for adults to teach them to overcome their fear of tests and to give them experience in testing exercises.

The black heritage series
The CBS television network came up with the idea of producing an educational series on black history. Because of previous work with Columbia, network people approached Winston Kirby, director of the university office of radio and television. At Kirby's suggestion, an eight-member advisory panel was set up, headed by Vincent Harding, professor of history and anthropology at Spellman College in Atlanta. Three members of the Columbia faculty, including the outspoken and popular professors James Shenton of history and Terence Hopkins of sociology, were included. In an unusual step, the non-Columbia members of the panel were paid $100 per meeting.

The CBS network made an investment of about $250,000, provided the facilities, the air time, the announcer, the producer, and the cameraman, and made efforts to employ minority-group technicians. Despite resistance from the Columbia administration, Kirby was able to get $20,000 from the Urban Center to handle travel expenses and consultant fees. Columbia later agreed to pay one person to produce the visual aids that might be desired by lecturers on the programs. Ewart Guinier of the Urban Center served the crucial role of mediator between Columbia and the somewhat suspicious non-Columbia members of the advisory panel. (The panel was so mistrustful that it hired its own attorney.) The advisory panel set up the course outline and invited the 31 lecturers, each of whom received $250 per lecture hour, about double the going rate for such activity.

By December 1968, most of the 108-part series was completed. On January 2, 1969, a public screening was held, at which time the three non-Columbia black advisory panel members — Vincent Harding, John Hendrik Clarke, and William Strickland — issued a letter of protest to CBS. They claimed:

1 The advisory board was consulted on only 25 percent of the series
2 The black cameraman was used only periodically
3 A black public relations firm should have been hired to promote the series in the community
4 The time of airing (before 9 A.M.) was bad
5 The panel was not consulted about the public screening

The protest was dealt with satisfactorily and the third demand was met — constituting the first time CBS had ever hired a public relations firm for a public service program. Controversy did not end, however, as Roy Wilkins publicly denounced the program for playing down the role of the NAACP and for expressing an extreme, militant point of view.

Columbia served primarily to convene and legitimate the program, although it also gave some money. The university faculty was generally cold to the endeavor and gave it no encouragement. Partly this was by design, as Shenton and Hopkins felt the series could be a showcase for young black academicians. The problems that later gave rise to the protest had been anticipated in the planning but were almost impossible to prevent. On the whole, the university's role was excellent, but only a few individuals participated.

Medical school programs

In addition to its famed Columbia-Presbyterian Hospital, Columbia became involved in providing medical services to the community in mid-1962 when it began a program of affiliation with Harlem Hospital, an antiquated facility in the middle of a low-income black community. The first step was Columbia's staffing of the Department of Psychiatry, and by December 1966 Columbia held nine affiliation contracts amounting to $8.5 million per year. At that time, almost all Department of Psychiatry directors were Columbia faculty members, the entire medical staff was from the College of Physicians and Surgeons or the School of Public Health, and the School of Social Work was providing all the social services. The affiliation was not without controversy.

Building on this program, the Urban Center granted $20,000 to start the Harlem Hospital Center School for Assistant Laboratory Technicians. It trained 20 community people (15 women and 5 men) as inhalation therapists, delivery room technicians, and other paraprofessionals. In an unrelated move, the Urban Center also provided $65,000 initial equity for a $3 million, 124-bed nursing home for low-income residents near Harlem Hospital.

SUMMARY Franklin Williams resigned as director of the Urban Center in November 1969 to become head of the Phelps-Stokes Fund. In announcing his resignation, he did not claim to have turned the university around, but he did offer a positive view of where the university was: "I am convinced that there has developed throughout this institution an increasing sensitivity to the problems of the people who are our neighbors and a spreading desire to be responsive and supportive to them."[1]

No one could deny that the university had made changes. Five new trustees were appointed in July 1969, including two blacks, two educators, and a diplomat. At the Urban Center's request, Columbia transferred a sizable deposit from a Morningside Heights bank to a Harlem bank, in 1968. A new, positive approach to physical expansion was clearly in evidence. In April 1968, John Telfer, formerly university planner at Michigan, became assistant vice-president for physical planning, Columbia's first real planner. The renowned architectural firm of I. M. Pei and Associates was commissioned to produce Columbia's first real plan. Pei was given unusual latitude because of the absence of any previous university plan; he was permitted to consult with anyone inside or outside the

[1] Cited in Williams, 1972, p. 1.

university. The community developed a trust in Pei. "He's head and shoulders above anyone eles in the field in social consciousness," said Telfer. In April 1969, President Cordier issued a policy statement repudiating the university's past opposition to public housing in Morningside Heights.

In the spring of 1970 Pei issued a report proposing complete utilization of the existing campus grounds by construction deeper and higher than previously envisioned, before expanding outward. The controversial gym is being built below ground. Pei also dealt imaginatively with the Pharmacy School site—a block located north and east of the campus that was originally purchased for the construction of new Pharmacy School facilities, which was never begun because of community opposition. Pei proposed a high-rise housing unit for dual use by the university and the community on the site. During demolition of part of the block, residents would be relocated in another part of the block. Community rents would be kept at public housing rates, while Columbia people would pay a high differential rate. Marie Runyon, a tenant leader, remarked, "Pei and his colleagues do give a damn. It's the first time in history that this has happened." Pei's plan was not the first in the area; in November 1968 Teachers College had announced plans for a similar dual-use tower in its expansion northward.

The physical expansion problem was not completely solved. Columbia still faced a tremendous space crunch arising from delayed construction of the School of International Affairs, the move of the School of Social Work to the Heights, condemnation of buildings housing five academic units, and conversion of 88 undergraduate rooms from doubles to singles. The proposed operation of a nuclear reactor, which the Engineering School constructed on the campus, has also elicited community furor because of possible hazards. But given Columbia's history, a remarkable amount of movement has occurred. Telfer says: "So much has been so long neglected here that I feel like I'm racing to catch up for three decades. Other universities moved ten or fifteen years ago to build up planning resources and staff. Columbia did not."

Changes in other areas of university life are not as evident as in the planning area. In curriculum study and minority recruitment, two areas in which Frank Williams felt the Urban Center's involvements were the most successful, the center has made barely perceptible waves. The community programs have had varied success. As Conrad Graves of the Urban Center says, "We have not really been able to change attitudes; rather, we have provided ways for those who were concerned to act. Maybe in the process of their doing things, others will change."

Probably the most valuable contribution of the Urban Center has been a catalytic one, using administrative personnel as liaisons between the baronies of the various schools, the community, and itself. Some schools, such as Social Work and Journalism, hardly needed a catalyst. Others, such as Arts and General Studies, needed primarily money—and more than the Urban Center gave them. Teachers College needed coordination. Still others, such as Law, Medicine, and the graduate faculties, did not seem to be sure what they needed.

As for the Urban Center, it faces an uncertain future under a new director, Lloyd Johnson. The Ford money is almost exhausted, and there is serious doubt that the university will provide it with the level of funds to which it has become accustomed. The center is still badly needed as both catalyst and liaison. The university cannot expect Ford or any other outside agency to save it again. As far as Columbia is concerned, "to turn around" must now become an intransitive rather than a transitive verb.

References

Avorn, Jerry L., and members of the staff of the Columbia Daily Spectator: *Up against the Ivy Wall,* Atheneum Publishers, New York, 1969.

Bell, Daniel: *The Reforming of General Education: The Columbia Experience in Its National Setting,* Columbia University Press, New York, 1966.

Berengarten, Sidney: *The Columbia School of Social Work, Report for the Years 1967–69,* report by the acting dean, the Columbia School of Social Work, New York, 1969.

Caplow, Theodore: *Urban and Minority Problems: A Brief Inventory of Columbia's Current Activities,* report submitted to the University Planning Committee, Columbia University, New York, Oct. 21, 1966.

Columbia College Tomorrow, a special report prepared by the Association of the Alumni of Columbia College, New York, 1969.

Cox Commission: *Crisis at Columbia: Report of the Fact-finding Commission Appointed to Investigate the Disturbances at Columbia University in April and May 1968,* Vintage Books, Random House, Inc., New York, 1968.

Faculty Civil Rights Group: *The Community and the Expansion of Columbia University,* Columbia University, New York, December 1967.

Frankel, Charles: *Education and the Barricades,* W. W. Norton & Company, Inc., New York, 1968.

The Human Uses of the University, report of the Urban Center Curriculum Project, Columbia University, New York, November 1969.

Isaacson, Margery, Doris Chrenstein, Elliot Rosen, Seddon R. Savage, and Robert H. Waldman: *Columbia and Unions: Past Policy and New Possibilities,* a report of the Columbia College Citizenship Council Committee for Research, Columbia University, New York, 1968.

Jencks, Christopher, and David Riesman: *The Academic Revolution,* Doubleday & Company, Inc., Garden City, N.Y., 1968.

Kolodny, Robert: *The East Harlem Urban Planning Studio: A Report of the First Year,* Columbia University, New York, April 1969.

Nash, George, and Cynthia Epstein: "Harlem Views Columbia University," *New York Magazine,* pp. 58–60, July 8, 1968.

Nash, George, and Patricia Nash: "Leads Columbia Could Have Followed," *New York Magazine,* pp. 38–41, June 3, 1968.

The Progress and Promise of Columbia University in the City of New York, trustees' report, Columbia University, New York, July 1967.

Rauch, Marc, Bob Feldman, and Art Leaderman: *Columbia and the Community: Past Policy and New Directions,* a report of the Columbia College Citizenship Council Committee for Research, Columbia University, New York, 1968.

Report of the President's Committee on Urban–Minority Problems, Columbia University, New York, June 15, 1967.

Ridgeway, James: *The Closed Corporation,* Random House, Inc., New York, 1968.

Rudolph, Frederick: *The American College and University,* Alfred A. Knopf, Inc., New York, 1965.

Terestman, Nettie: *Report on Black Recruitment and Enrollment and the Urban Center's Involvement,* Columbia University, New York, 1969.

Toward Equal Educational Opportunity in the Urban Setting: Report on the Activities of the Urban Center in Support of Increased Minority Student Enrollment, Columbia University, New York, December 1969.

Urban Center: *Annual Report,* Columbia University, New York, June 1969.

Who Rules Columbia? prepared by the North American Congress on Latin America, New York, 1968.

Williams, Franklin: Letter to Andrew Cordier, dean, *Columbia University News Letter,* vol. 11, no. 11, p. 1, Dec. 8, 1969.

9. Wayne State: The Urban University

by Dan Waldorf

Like many other cities in America, Detroit, the site of Wayne State University, has experienced a mass exodus of its affluent, white citizens from the central city to its suburbs. Those left behind are, in large part, poor blacks, many of whom are recent migrants from the South. With the black migration has come an increase in the demand for services. With the white exodus has come a decline in taxes and revenues that has curtailed many services previously provided by the city. The result has been a myriad of social problems. Health problems have increased, as doctors have moved to suburban areas; the number of housing units has declined because of clearing for freeways and urban renewal, as more and better housing is needed; crime rates have increased; and persons long denied the opportunity for education are increasingly discontented with the extent and quality of education now available.

The city of Detroit has not been able to deal with these problems. In some ways, it seems to be growing worse, not better. It is possible, however, that some of Detroit's problems will eventually be solved and that a new urban atmosphere may evolve. If there is hope for a solution, part of it emanates from the efforts being made by the administration, faculty, and students of Wayne State University to attack social problems. Few universities have seen and met the challenges presented by urban problems as Wayne State has. It seems that nearly every one of its schools and departments has someone with a social conscience who is attacking the problem of living in Detroit. Examples are innumerable and it is difficult to know where to begin describing the many ways in which Wayne State is serving its community. Since drug abuse is a major current problem, I will start with that area.

Detroit, New York City, Los Angeles, and Chicago are considered to have large numbers of heroin addicts. The Wayne State Medical School started a program at Detroit General Hospital to treat heroin addiction with the synthetic narcotic methadone. Previously, aside from detoxification treatment, there had been only sporadic efforts to treat addiction in Detroit.

Ronald Krome, who had worked with narcotic addicts at the U.S. Public Health Hospital in Lexington, Kentucky, was responsible for starting the program. Along with his other duties (as Detroit General's director of emergency services and assistant professor of surgery at the Wayne State School of Medicine), he undertook this program, with very little money (overtime pay for two nurses and a salary for a counselor who was an ex-addict) but some hope of additional funds from the city of Detroit.

The unusual thing about the program was that it was operated very matter-of-factly as a part of the normal services of Detroit General Hospital with its small staff and funding. The program was discontinued in November 1970 when the city failed to provide financial support. It illustrates that not all of Wayne State's efforts have been successful.

The dean of the College of Pharmacy, Martin Barr, initiated another effort: the drug education prevention program. He says,

I got started on the idea one night at Southfield. I was in the audience of a panel discussion about drugs. There was a panel of five persons and they terrified the whole audience with horror stories. I knew then that there had to be other approaches, and that kicked off our whole program. I got both students and faculty involved in it; this year [1969–70] we have 20 students and 5 faculty members. They are all volunteers. We send someone out almost every day; last year we spoke to about 50,000 persons. . . . We try to touch on all aspects of the problem—biochemistry, social, psychological, legal, etc. Naturally, the approach is tailored to the prospective participants: parents and professionals want facts and descriptions of symptoms to detect drug abuse; students want persons who can talk from their own experience. Students speak to students, faculty to adults. What we try to get across is a healthy respect for the short- and long-term effects of drugs. In addition, we are also training others (usually teachers) who will in turn go into schools. This year we enrolled 55 graduate teachers in a credit course on basic pharmacological concepts of drug abuse.

Barr and his associates recognize the problems of using traditional educational approaches to teach prevention of drug abuse.

They are attempting to forge new techniques and approaches that will be more effective.

CONSUMER EDUCATION

Wayne State's consumer education project was started in 1967 by Roberta McBride, the librarian of the university's Archives of Labor History and Urban Affairs. She is described by those who know her as quietly persistent. The consumer education courses she has put together are very well organized and wide-ranging.

The program used not only Wayne State faculty members but also experts from Michigan State's University Extension Service, the Credit Union League of Michigan, and local organizations. Students were usually poor persons from more than 50 participating organizations. The program has been particularly effective in reaching blacks. What sets the project apart is that each of the participants, after the course of study (45 weekly meetings), is supposed to go back to his local community and teach a similar course. Using this multiplier effect, the project reached considerably larger numbers than the 50 persons enrolled.

Mrs. McBride was enthusiastic about the class participation. She said that at least 20 or 30 persons showed up each week even during the coldest weather. Initially the courses were to be held in the community on the premises of the participating agencies. But the participants liked coming to the university, and the university liked having them, so classes were held in very pleasant, comfortable classrooms at the university conference center. Out of this pilot program has grown a consumer education program for credit to be operated in 10 centers by a community organization called New Detroit, Inc.

COMMUNITY EXTENSION CENTERS

Another imaginative program that is attempting to make university facilities available to black inner-city residents is the new Community Extension Center program in the Division of Urban Extension. Prior to 1968, Urban Extension operated primarily in the white suburban noose surrounding Detroit, rather than in the central city. Decentralization of the Urban Extension facilities was proposed by Dean Hamilton Stillwell (now at Rutgers University) as a means of "bringing University Extension back home to the inner city by setting up centers in several black communities."

The initial plans for the program were developed by a black administrator, Conrad Mallett, who is highly regarded in Detroit because of his work with former Mayor Cavanagh and as the former director of the Detroit Housing Commission. Mallett then went on to become director of Wayne State's Office of Neighborhood Relations. The Community Extension Center program was implemented by Mallett's successor, Hartford Smith, Jr., a bearded black man who is an assistant professor in Wayne's School of Social Work.

Smith was responsible for opening the first Community Extension Center. He undertook a study of several city neighborhoods and finally chose to locate the first center in one of the poorest sections of the city, a Model Neighborhood area on the east side. The facility is a large former parochial school. An advisory board made up of community residents was selected, and the board members drew up the first operational plan for the center. The overall plan called for a multipurpose neighborhood center that would house a variety of educational, cultural, and recreational programs. The recreation component was the starting point because of the urgent and immediate need for it in the hot summer months just ahead. Smith said:

It must be realized that this was more than just another summer recreation program. First, it was an attempt to stick to the wise philosophy of starting where the people are; and second, it was made clear by the residents that it should be recreation with a purpose—recreation that could be used to get people involved in doing something about conditions affecting them. We also wanted to encourage them to participate in the educational and cultural programs being planned for the Center.

In the fall of 1969, the center started its second stage of development by offering courses at the college level. These were basic courses: English composition and literature, sociology and social problems, and introductory psychology. All were taught by regular Wayne State faculty selected by Smith's division. There was also a noncredit community service course for community leaders, which attempted to relate various urban problems—such as drug abuse, housing, and welfare—to community law.

Initial efforts to start noncredit community courses did not meet with overwhelming success. Smith explained:

We made a few mistakes last year. We didn't know the psychology of charging fees in this community. Here it was, we were offering courses free, and they had a peculiar philosophy that shot us down. I guess they felt: "If it's worth a damn, it has to be worth at least a buck—you get nothing free in this world." So we revamped the whole thing, charged $5, and got two community leaders to sign up for the course. In addition, there were strong negative feelings about noncredit programs because of a history of poor acceptance by employers.

In addition to the credit and noncredit courses, there were informal courses that generally took the form of tutorials, in reading, in mathematics, and as refreshers for people planning to take the High School Equivalency tests. To illustrate how one person got into such a course, Professor Smith told this story:

We have this one kid, you know, a real tough dude. He's about 17 years old, out of school, and has raised a lot of hell in the community and in our recreation program. A couple of staff members saw him packing a rod before we made our "no weapons" rule. On a couple of occasions he had threatened to close down the Center. He was banned for a month, but gradually he has come to accept the Center's rules and discipline. One day recently, he came to me and asked if he could sign up for a tutorial in the High School Equivalency course so that he might eventually get into some college credit courses at the Center.

I think having the rec program like we do can encourage many persons like this one to get started taking courses, especially when they are both offered in the same plant and not across town in alien country.

In addition to these activities, the center has a separate contract with a group of welfare mothers who are trying to get themselves off welfare by learning typing and stenography. There is a large demand for such workers that is not being met in Detroit. A well-equipped clerical laboratory facility was made available by the Department of Business Education on Wayne's main campus. During the first term, 40 women signed up and attended regularly. Professor Smith explained how this project led into another:

The need of this group of welfare mothers for some kind of day care for their children while the mothers are in class caused us to start to think about developing some self-sustaining day-care units which would allow persons participating in the programs to bring children along with them and not have to worry about getting a baby-sitter. Things aren't always as neat, well-ordered, or easily tied into an educational ball; when you go into a community where there are a lot of needs you have to try to relate your program to this whole range of needs. If what they need is X and you are offering Y, you simply aren't responding to them appropriately. At a university, things have to fit into nice, neat places, but that isn't where the real world is.

The problems of setting up such a program are continuous, according to the director:

There's no problem getting people into the Center—and especially kids—because of the gym. Our real problem is getting them there in some order. We were pretty loose at first—too loose, I'm sure—and we had a crisis a day. Someone was always confronting us with something. Many of the problems and conflicts of the larger community were becoming a part of the Center as the Center became more a part of the community. There are many "tests" and battles for control. For instance, one day a group of tough dudes came into the Center Director's office, came in and told him that they were planning to take over the place and if he didn't let them take it over, they were going to bomb it down. Well, he let them talk for a while and then told them that like any other place, there were certain rules about using the Center, and then he told them why and laid it out for them—one, two, three, four. . . . Well, they made some grumbling noises, said they were going to burn it down, and left. But they started living with the rules eventually.

The factor that was most impressive was the generally loose and open attitude of the center staff, which allowed it to respond to suggestions made by the people who used the facilities.

By the spring of 1971, enrollment had grown to 200 students in college credit courses, with a vastly increased number and range of course choices, still taught by Wayne State faculty. After 12 hours of B work or 16 hours of C work, students may and are encouraged to transfer to the main campus. Some of the original students from the center and regular Wayne State students serve as paid team leaders, to help new center students make the transition to full campus work. About 80 students, including a welfare mother who has eight children, have transferred to the main campus for regular college-degree work.

The center has developed a range of courses for paraprofessionals working in community service agencies in the ghetto. It has developed mechanisms for providing high school completion work and for providing technical orientation and training for 125 high school dropouts. There are 50 adults attending a similar basic educational high school completion program at night. Many of these persons also may move on to the college credit track.

In addition, Smith and his staff have arranged for community groups actually to run certain aspects of the center's program. For example, a cooperative called Project C.H.I.L.D. that is organized and operated by citizens now manages day-care programs. The Payne Athletic Association, a similar citizens' group, operates basketball and baseball leagues through the center. Both groups received technical assistance from the center staff.

The Community Extension Center is meeting its stated goal of becoming a "cultural hub in the community" by presenting plays, talent shows, educational field trips, special community-related workshops and conferences, and a speakers' program. It encourages the development of drama clubs etc. for the young. If its programming continues at its present pace, the East Side Center will have to expand its present facilities.

SPECIAL STUDENT SERVICE PROGRAMS During the 1967–68 academic year, the undergraduate black population at Wayne State University was 8.8 percent of the 22,600 students. This was the highest percentage of black undergraduates for any large, publicly supported college or university in the United States. By 1970–71 black graduate and undergraduate students accounted for 15.6 percent of the student body. The increase was the result of a concerted effort by the university to make itself more available to its neighbors.

Much of the increase in black student enrollment at Wayne is directly attributable to the Special Student Service Programs (SSSP), a general title under which fall several programs, including the Higher Education Opportunities Committee (HEOC), which is the Talent Search program at Wayne State. The HEOC was started in 1963 by Wayne faculty and Detroit citizens to provide financial support for needy but academically successful black graduates of Detroit high schools. Upward Bound, also under SSSP, was started at Wayne in 1966. It was cited in a national evaluation by Greenleigh Associates in 1969 as the operational model for all Upward Bound programs in the country. The third major SSSP program is Project 350, a thriving program built during 1968–69 from two experimental efforts in 1967–68 that were informally designated Project 300 and Project 50 for the number of students in each one.

Project 300 was Wayne's first major experimental admissions program. The university relaxed its admissions policies and accepted 300 applicants who had been denied admission on their first try and whose grade point averages were 2.0 to 2.3—just below the customary GPA requirement. Referred to as the "cream of the rejects," these students were selected from around the state solely on the basis of their GPAs; there was a preponderance of suburban, white students. Graduates from Detroit's inner-city high schools accounted for only about 20 percent of this group.

That same summer, Project 50 was persuaded into being by the then assistant dean of students, Murray Jackson, and the then director of HEOC Noah Brown, Jr. (Brown became director of Special Student Service Programs in the fall of 1968, and in July 1970 he was named vice-president for student affairs.) Both Jackson and Brown are native Detroiters, black, and very strong-minded. They saw that if the GPA was used as the only guide to selection, students from the predominantly black high schools in Detroit's central city would be excluded. The students in Project 50 were chosen more or less randomly by Jackson and Brown. There were actually 52 students, 50 of them black.

The philosophy and leadership of Project 50 and Project 300 were merged in October of 1968, and Project 350 was created (or re-created) under drastically changed selection and program guidelines for the 1969–70 school year. The project has maintained its annual admission level of 350 students, and by the summer of 1971 the total number of students admitted under this special effort had reached 1,400.

Noah Brown convened a Campus Planning Committee for special programs, composed of representatives from a variety of units related to student personnel services and academic instruction. This conglomerate of faculty members, administrators, and students continues to mastermind the programming activities of the Special Student Service Programs division.

Brown also established a Community Advisory Committee on Special Student Programs and Summer Job Placement. It is composed of citizens representing a wide range of Detroit concerns: the municipal department of parks and recreation, a major public housing project, the city's poverty program umbrella agency, public and parochial high school teachers and principals, the Detroit Board of Education, the Varsity Club (black athletes), and a unique nonprofit job placement agency called the Volunteer Placement Corps. This committee is responsible each year for identifying and recruiting 50 of the 350 students from across its reach of community contacts, and for helping to find jobs and to provide job counseling for all project students throughout their university careers.

With the extremely active assistance of these two broad-based committees, Brown began to recruit heavily from several designated poverty areas. Concentrating recruitment in target areas allows Wayne to draw upon a population of students almost universally overlooked by recruiters from other colleges and universities. The criteria used to identify an area as a target include family income level, level of unemployment, high school drop-out rate, and ethnic composition. Consideration of these data, along with the individual student's grade record in high school, his motivation and aspirations as identified by teachers and counselors, and his results on the standard admission tests, gives Wayne a loosely woven but relatively coherent set of guidelines for recruitment.

Noah Brown is an amazing man, who absolutely bubbles with energy and enthusiasm for his work. He is completely committed to the job of getting black and other minority students into Wayne State and making sure that they have the best chance to stay there until they finish whatever course they are pursuing.

Physically Brown is a large, robust man who does not give the impression that he was a star basketball player at Wayne State after his World War II army service. But from his enthusiasm it is easy to tell what kind of player he was—full of hustle, always down the court first on the fast break. He has a great gift for "turning people on" to his ideas. Everyone on his staff is said to be "hooked" on him and on the project. Brown provides this inspiration in several ways—as an energetic director, as a sympathetic, warm person, and as an impassioned and effective speaker with many of the talents of an old-style black preacher.

By 1969–70, the second year of Project 350, Brown had things well organized. All 350 places were filled. There were 250 marginal students and 100 high-risk students. The majority were black. In addition, Brown was able to recruit an additional 67 students, on very short notice, for a similar program at Michigan State University.

Counseling and tutoring were expanded during the second year of the program. Counseling is aggressive and mandatory. Students in Project 350 are contacted every week individually either in person or by telephone. Each of the counseling sessions is recorded on a special report sheet so that there is very close monitoring and follow-up of each student's progress, The counselor-student ratio is 1 to 60, and each counselor stays with the same student throughout the year in order to maintain continuity and to establish the maximum possible personal relationship.

In addition to scheduled counseling, there is a tutorial center where students may go for assistance either when they think they need it or when they are referred by their counselors. Most of the tutors and counselors are black and are students who themselves entered the university through special admission programs. Many of the tutors are graduate fellows who are assigned to tutoring positions by their instructional departments.

The problem—not only at Wayne, but at schools all over the country that recruit large numbers of low-income students—is that the number of such students is increasing, as they begin to believe the "educational opportunity" message—a very wholesome sign for higher education in general—just at the time when the sources and amounts of financial assistance for these students are diminishing. Wayne, like many other urban institutions, is left holding the bag. The federal aid to needy students dwindles steadily, almost a reverse reflection of the rising numbers knocking at admissions office doors.

The specially admitted black students had to make some adjustments to integrated classroom situations where black students were in the minority. Marjorie Edwards, the academic advisor for special programs, tells of one first-year student who apparently never had been in such a classroom. At Wayne, she was attending an introductory social science class in which there were only six or seven black students. The black and the white students tended to sit apart from each other. The girl informed Miss Edwards that her instructor was a racist and was not concerned about black students; he was not addressing his lectures to all students but only to the white students, she said. The examples the instructor used in class applied primarily to the white students, and he tended to fix his eyes in only one area of the classroom—not the area where the black students were sitting. The student took this very personally.

Miss Edwards tried to analyze the situation, being sure not to take sides, and told the girl to try an experiment: she should take a seat in an area of the classroom away from the other black students and observe whether the instructor still seemed to address his lecture and discussion only to the white students. The student was also firmly reminded that she had paid her tuition for that class and that she belonged there. She was encouraged to talk to her classmates, and she was told to return if she still felt she had a problem after trying what was suggested. The student returned at the end of the quarter and told Miss Edwards that her fears were unfounded and that she had talked to the instructor, who she decided really was concerned about all the students in his class.

In the academic year 1968–69 the median grade point average for all special students was 2.0, but six had averages of 3.0 or better. The best grades were in English and psychology. The general trend is for all students to improve their grades as they learn better how to study and become accustomed to university life.

THE COOPERATIVE WORK AND STUDY EDUCATIONAL PROGRAM
Another program Wayne State established primarily to assist black students is the Cooperative Work and Study program. This was instigated by Benson Manlove, a tall, confident, black man who said he was probably destined to become a pimp or street hustler until he went to college. While a senior in the School of Business Administration, he went to the president with his observation that there were very few black students in the Business School and in the College of Engineering; he said he wanted to work on plans to get more black students into these two schools particularly. One of his plans was the co-op program of alternating terms of work and school. President Keast liked Manlove and his ideas, and appointed him assistant to the president practically on the spot, in the summer of 1968.

The co-op program opened the next summer with 20 students. It was enlarged in the fall to 100 students and added another 80 in the winter. Manlove's goal of 200 students during the first year was met.

Students may enter the co-op program after they have completed 80 hours of credit with at least a 2.0 grade point average. The majority of the students now in the program were already enrolled at Wayne State before joining the co-op program, but considerable efforts were made in planning for the second year to recruit from community colleges in the Detroit area. The program takes five years to complete, and many students are resistant to the idea of such a long commitment, despite the fact that the average student at Wayne State takes five years to get an undergraduate degree.

Students in the program are enthusiastic about the co-op idea. A group interview was held with five black students. A slim, pretty girl about twenty-five years old, who had been at Wayne State for six years working part time toward her degree in accounting, said she felt a certain relief after joining the co-op:

Co-op is a lot better, you know—you're not as pushed. When I was working at Wayne and going to school, too, I never felt like a student. I was always having to rush here and do this, rush there and do that. I was busy all the time, but now I've got time to relax and to do some things besides working and studying.

At her co-op placement she earned $600 a month, which was considerably more than she earned working part time. This money allowed her to have more leisure and to do things that less financially pressed students do.

Manlove's enthusiasm for the co-op plan is so great that he organized the National Cooperative Education Association to encourage the development of similar programs in black colleges, mostly in the South.

An interesting outcome of Manlove's interest and activity in the College of Engineering and the School of Business Administration is that black students have established their own associations there that are independent of the larger University Association of Black Students. They were initiated with the goal of cutting down the attrition rate of black students, and they are organized and focused around vocational and professional interests rather than on broad political and black studies interests.

SUMMER SCIENCE RESEARCH PROGRAM Programs for poor, underprivileged, inner-city children appear in unexpected places at Wayne State—such as the physics department. Persons with social consciences are not restricted to any one department at Wayne. They seem to abound everywhere.

The physics department's Summer Science Research program attempts to bring relatively high-ability high school juniors and seniors from the inner city into physical science laboratories as interns, where they work with a graduate research assistant under direct supervision of a professor. The intern works seven hours a day, five days a week, in the laboratory, and attends a weekly lecture series given by various professors in the department. There is a specific attempt to stay away from a schoollike atmosphere (the students need a change after 10 months in school) and a strong emphasis on real work situations that allow the participants to stretch beyond their present levels of functioning.

This is not a make-work program. From its inception, it was conceived to assist the physics department as well as the interns. Leonard Roellig, the thoughtful and able director of the project, said that he continually stresses to professors who request interns that they need to make the work interesting and take time to teach the interns the specific tasks they must learn in order to do the jobs.

The graduate student under whom the intern works serves as a link between the intern and the professor. The intern works with the graduate student in a close, day-to-day relationship, and it is expected that the graduate student will take a personal interest in the laboratory intern and make a special effort to get to know him or her. Graduate students are encouraged to take the interns to the student center, to show them around the campus, to socialize with them informally, and generally to serve as role models.

Professor Roellig said of the high school students:

Most of the interns who come to the program have never known a college-educated individual *as a person,* in contrast to youth of today's middle-class suburbia who have friends, relatives, and neighbors who have successfully completed college. Our program provides the opportunity for the interns to develop a close personal relationship with college people and at the same time, it gives them the opportunity to learn what it is like to be a research physicist, chemist, or biologist. Generally, the work is varied; it depends upon the specific lab and what tasks have to be done. Students may analyze data, make measurements, build apparatus, take field trips, etc.

Results of the Summer Science Research program have been most encouraging. Roellig sent cards to the first 20 students who participated in the 1967 program asking them to come to a group meeting at Wayne State. Of the 13 who came to the meeting 12 were in or had been accepted by some college or university; many felt they had been able to get scholarships because of their participation in the program. Professors in the program were helpful in writing recommendations for individual interns, based on their knowledge of the students' abilities and work habits.

Funding for the program has come from three sources: Neighborhood Youth Corps, New Detroit, Inc. (an agency of local businessmen and civic leaders that grew out of the ashes of the 1967 riots), and Wayne State itself.

SOCIAL WORK STUDENT PLACEMENTS Traditionally, schools of social work have placed graduate students in social agencies to learn case work, psychiatric social work, group work, or community organization as student-practitioners under supervision. More recently, there has been a heavy increase in interest in the community social work component. Wayne State's School of Social Work has experienced this shift of emphasis, and, as is characteristic of the whole university, it has taken the idea much farther. The Wayne innovation is to place graduate students in community organization in the offices of politicians, to serve as legislative ombudsmen who deal with problems of the inner city and the poor.

This program began in September 1966 with placements to four legislators—one congressman, two state legislators, and a Detroit common councilman. By the 1969–70 school year, eleven students were being placed with six legislators and three legislative agencies. Students spend three days a week in the office of the legislator and two days in class. The program covers a whole school year.

The experiences of students as described in a group interview were very illuminating:

Three of the students—William Long, Jewell Burdette, and Robert Santos —were, with one of the faculty members, Assistant Professor William Iverson, working in the office of Congressman John Conyers, Jr. The principal duties of the three placements were to handle constituents' complaints. Whenever a constituent either writes or calls Congressman Conyers about a specific grievance, it is the intern's job to learn the specifics of the particular complaint and to make some effort to satisfy the constituent. Complaints ranged from the very personal—a man trying to get unemployment benefits after being told twice by the employment office that he didn't qualify—to the larger national issues such as the draft, the war in Vietnam, urban environment, big city problems, etc.

The students had direct but infrequent access to the Congressman himself, but all worked very closely with members of his staff in his local Detroit office.

In addition to the routine work of handling constituent complaints, each of the three specialized in specific projects with which the Congressman was working. For example, Robert Santos had been working extensively with consumer groups on consumer fraud. One of the initial efforts of this special project was to work with the United Farm Workers to stage a boycott of grapes picked by non-union workers—the grapes were being sold in certain of the larger supermarkets. This led to other efforts concerning specific consumer problems.

None of the three thought that he was too effective in influencing either the Congressman or his staff, but felt that the experience was worth it because it allowed an opportunity to see how the political scene was run and how he could be more effective as a social worker and as a citizen.

The approach to political placements generally is bipartisan, although the values and social philosophy of the legislators are considered in the placements. It is generally understood by the students and by the host legislators that the students are to deal with issues that are particularly relevant to social policy.

Limits of space do not allow me to describe other programs of the School of Social Work, but it, like nearly all schools at Wayne State, is active in a variety of projects that relate to the inner city and to the problems of the poor and the black communities.

THE CENTER FOR URBAN STUDIES Not everything goes well at Wayne. One of the major projects through which President Keast tried to give emphasis and focus to the urban involvement at Wayne had serious internal and external problems and a recent change in leadership. The problems occurred in the Center for Urban Studies, which was established in 1968 "to draw all the major schools, colleges, and divisions into a flexible and increasingly maturing network recognizing *both* their independence and their interdependence, and utilizing both in enhancing their capabilities for response to urbanization."

The center is responsible for four basic areas: research, education, international urban studies, and community activities. According to Richard Simmons, Jr., an associate director of the center and an associate professor in the School of Social Work, ". . . it's community activity (throughout the University) that will be the cutting edge. . . . That will be the difference between the Center for Urban Studies at Wayne—a center that wants to get things done and to work in the local community—and institutes at other universities formed around urban problems."

The center was given substantial support, funds, and staff by the university to accomplish its goals. A full-time director was named in January 1969, and during its first year of operation a good deal was accomplished. The most notable achievements were an exchange program of European urban planners, the publication of a fact book of planning data for Detroit, a conference of urban studies directors from all around the country, a conference on new towns, and development of a model to revitalize Detroit's Woodward-Cass corridor (the area in which the university is situated). There were, however, problems arising from the personality of the director, and he engendered fears that the center would attempt to coordinate all urban involvement at the university. Such involvement was just too diffuse and complex to be coordinated.

The four divisions of the center worked well enough in their own spheres but did not mesh too well with each other. The first director of the center, who left in 1970, was an interesting and productive scholar, but he was not able to provide the administrative glue that would have given the four divisions shared goals and concerns. Consequently, the parts tended to compete with each other, wasting much time and energy, although many of their individual projects were excellent.

The community activities division, under Professor Simmons, was asked to mediate when a Catholic church activities building in St. Peter Claver parish was being taken from the jurisdiction of the archdiocese and the parish and given to United Community Services, which had, in fact, been providing most if not all of its support over the last few years. This was one of those touchy situations in which the neighborhood residents wanted, and felt demonstrably justified in taking over complete control of facility, since they were the ones using it, but the parish was reluctant to let go of its old-style "lady bountiful" control over the facility, out of genuine fear for the building's survival and proper use. Professor Simmons, working patiently over a long period, provided negotiating opportunities and guidelines for all the parties, and slowly but surely the group came to an agreement fully satisfactory to both sides. The measure of his success (which he claims for the university, since his work was sanctioned by the university) is that at the very end of the process some of the original board members from the parish were asked—unanimously—by the community to continue as members of the newly revised and reorganized board of the center.

Jack Fisher directed the international urban studies division's American-Yugoslav project. Although much of the activity took place in Yugoslavia, not in Detroit, Yugoslavs are now almost fixtures on the campus of Wayne. Part of the program brings graduate students, called junior fellows, from both Eastern and Western Europe—Yugoslavia, Austria, Czechoslovakia, Germany, Italy, France, and England—to Wayne for a 10-month period of study and research in the Detroit urban region. Others, who are full-fledged professionals, called senior fellows, come for one quarter at a time to teach courses or to supervise research projects. This very successful program has had fiscal support from the Ford Foundation and continuous endorsement by the U.S. Department of State and by the national governments of the countries represented.

WAYNE'S URBAN EMPHASIS Wayne State's involvement with the problems of the city is long-standing. It seems to be an inherited tradition. Before becoming a large university, it was a collection of municipal colleges with a strong community orientation (a so-called streetcar college). The orientation has not changed despite the many changes that have accompanied the university's rapid growth. While Wayne State is no longer a prototype community college, it is definitely involved in the community—educating its citizens and providing services to its neighbors.

Both the past and the present leadership at Wayne have carried on the tradition of urban involvement. President William Keast (who retired in June 1971) carried Wayne's tradition further by making urban involvement the major focus of the entire university. Keast's energy belied his shock of white hair. In a 1967 address to the university faculty, he proposed that Wayne State should "be the nation's unique urban university," and he envisioned "a day when other institutions will look to us for the new patterns by which universities will help create a more humane urban society."

This goal of the university was to be attained by

1 modifying admissions policies and encouraging minority student enroll-ment among both undergraduates and graduate students

2 developing new methods of measuring and rewarding promise and high competence in teaching and distinguished service to the community, as well as scholarship and research

3 providing needed services to the community wherever possible, particularly through such agencies as the Center for Urban Studies and the Community Extension Center program

One year after Keast's talk, his administration documented what it was doing in an illustrated publication, *Wayne and the Inner City: A Survey of Urban Concern.*

Wayne has not by any means suspended the usual academic standards for judging competence (the publish-or-perish edict), and there are problems throughout the university of the more traditional kind. Richard Simmons of the Center for Urban Studies explained:

There are, and will be problems—and we don't minimize them for a min-ute—because community service just doesn't figure in any university re-ward system. You're not going to get promoted for all those meetings you attend in the local community or for anything that you might do out there. The only place in the University where I see this reward system breaking down is, perhaps, in the School of Social Work, which has been more in-volved with community activities and community serivce than any other single school at the University—but even there, you more or less have to publish or perish.

There exists a climate at Wayne State that has allowed standards to be modified, if not changed altogether. Persons are judged by the service they perform for the community, but they also are judged by traditional standards. Professor Roellig may get recognition at Wayne State for his fine program to educate the inner-city science student, but he will not be recognized by the larger physics and science communities unless he also does the things they expect of him. Until the larger academic system changes, Wayne will be something of an anomaly.

This limited description of Wayne State's urban involvement has covered only a fraction of the programs. It seems that President Keast's goal of total urban involvement has been realized. There is no more urban-related university than Wayne State, and the timing and innovativeness of its programs, in addition to their breadth and depth, are unusual.

Reference

Wayne and the Inner City: A Survey of Urban Concern, university brochure, Wayne State University, Detroit, 1968.

10. *Background*

An aim of this book has been to demonstrate that institutions of higher education have a great deal to contribute to the solution of urban, community, and minority-group problems. By presenting case studies we have outlined the methods in which institutions of higher education can become involved, and we have included both good and bad examples of such involvement. Now we will examine academic thinking on the subject of university urban involvement.

Whether colleges should attempt to become involved in providing services and solving problems is seen by many students of higher education as a controversial subject. Two polar positions have been identified—the case for involvement as advocated by John W. Gardner, head of Common Cause and former Secretary of Health, Education, and Welfare, and the case for maintenance of the ivory tower as advocated by Jacques Barzun, former provost of Columbia University. These positions make good journalistic copy, but they are oversimplifications, and they do not represent the real views of the authors.

There really is no debate about whether institutions of higher education should be involved in the urban crisis—all the prominent people who have discussed the subject agree that they should be. The debate revolves instead around the manner and style of involvement and the criteria for deciding whether a given university should attempt a given project.

At least four separate positions have been taken, and they do not necessarily conflict with each other. They are:

1 Involvement should be increased.

2 Special types of institutions of higher education should be created to deal with special types of urban problems.

3 Institutions of higher education have too many major problems, as they are presently constituted, to permit them to deal effectively with the problems of cities. They should put their own houses in order first.

4 There are limits to the possible involvements of colleges and universities in dealing with the urban crisis—especially when it comes to rendering services.

INVOLVEMENT INCREASED

John Gardner, addressing college presidents assembled for the annual convention of the American Council on Education in October 1968, indicted the universities for inaction:

> The colleges and universities of this country have not responded impressively to the urban crisis. They have been notably laggard. I know this comes as no news to you because many of you have spoken to me about it, and expressed your concern. There is, of course, a great amount of activity going on in colleges and universities that has the word "urban" attached. But my conversations with many of you indicate that you are not satisfied with the quality of those activities, and I share your view. I need not tell you of the shortcomings of the typical urban affairs center. Much of what they are doing today can only be described as "dabbling." Many are re-inventing the wheel and not doing a very good job of it. Very few have pursued any aspect of the subject with the intellectual rigor it requires (Gardner, 1969)

Gardner went on to suggest that the universities form urban task forces consisting of representatives of the students, faculty, trustees, and administration, together with representatives from their immediate neighborhoods. He stressed that the greatest resource the universities had at their command was today's students with activist inclinations. "They are seeking an outlet for their idealism. They have the impatience that makes for social renewal. They have a role to play" (Gardner, 1969).

In his book *Excellence* (1961), Gardner talked of the important role of education in preparing the citizens of an industrial nation for the competence needed in a complex society. He paid particular attention to the bottlenecks that prevent those who are lower in the social structure from achieving competence. The greatest crime of omission of educational institutions would be to allow wasted potential. He spoke particularly of the problems of blacks:

> A leading educator said recently, "Any Negro who is qualified can get a college education." The statement is approximately true but dodges the big issue. The fate of most talented Negro children is sealed long, long before

college. . . . Most Negro children with the intellectual capacity for higher education will fall by the wayside long before they get there (Gardner, 1961).

Another person to urge the increased involvement of institutions of higher education in the urban crisis is William Birenbaum, author of *Overlive* (1968) and president of Staten Island Community College:

The American university exerts a new kind of institutional power, a power flowing from its possession of extensive properties and huge material wealth, from its capacity to withhold or to give strategic services, from its willingness or reluctance to respond to the pressures and problems besetting the other primary power centers, from the quality and character of its responses. It leads because of what it does or does not do in the classroom and beyond it. But it also leads actively in the vital arenas far beyond the classroom and its own campus.

. . . Traditional notions about scholarly detachment, the meaning of "objectivity," the necessity for a disconnection between academic thought and social action, old ideas about how the human learns, the retreat from the streets of the city into the superblock campuses, the ways talent may or should be used—all of these and more deserve an intensive, fresh look. . . . The university can no longer avoid the risks of taking positions on the conduct and goals which it has chosen to wheel and deal. Indeed it has no choice about this. So long as it chooses to wheel and deal in the maintenance and extension of its own power, it takes risks—whether it consciously supports and approves the status quo or not. The twilight of an older academic era cannot be conjured away. The sun has set. No critique of the American university can go far in the absence of a confrontation with the society in which the academic institution is a power partner (Birenbaum, 1968, pp. 70–71).

Birenbaum also strongly favors the extension of educational opportunity:

The educational problems of the young black people in our cities represent a very special challenge to our colleges and universities. Large numbers of these young people must now be prepared to leapfrog over the dead-end, lower-level economic openings into the key professional and managerial command posts in the economy. They must be equipped to do this notwithstanding the educational damage done to them in their lower schools, not-

withstanding the distortions of life experience imposed upon them by growing up in the ghettos (Birenbaum, 1969).

Birenbaum speaks at length of the need for educational reform:

> There is no more important dimension to the education of the college stu-
> dent than the experience of being free in the regulation of his personal life
> and with regard to the public affairs of his community. . . . In freedom
> education, the learning community is itself the essential laboratory. Until
> this fact is recognized by those who teach and administer in universities,
> there will be more rather than less student unrest and discontent and there
> should be. The students are potentially the most powerful spearhead for the
> reform of the academic community. For them, the most vital issues of the
> community's life are not salary schedules, rank and promotion, tenure,
> status, and prestige. For them, the over-riding issue is the redistribution of
> power in the community in order to implement goals bearing upon the way
> they will live. The student unrest, whether expressed in regard to Vietnam,
> civil rights, General Hershey, or Dow Chemical, is really about educa-
> tion. . . . Student restiveness on campuses across the land is partially a
> reaction against the insular, detached and rigid attitude toward higher
> education so many of our universities represent. These young adults come
> to the colleges prepared to grow, seeking new connections in thought and
> through experience—between thought and experience—only to find recep-
> tions which underestimate or misjudge the range and significance of their
> past experience and their capacity to grow (Birenbaum, 1968, p. 148).

SPECIAL
INSTITUTIONS
In a speech at City College in New York in October 1967, Clark
Kerr, former president of the University of California and now
chairman of the Carnegie Commission on Higher Education, called
for the creation, with federal assistance, of urban-grant universities
in all cities with populations of 250,000 or more. These urban-grant
universities would focus on the cities in the same fashion that the
land-grant universities focused on rural and agricultural problems.
They would train and deploy specific urban agents. For example,
school agents, who are specialists in problem areas such as language, would take their expertise to the city's public schools. The
course work would not be restricted to city problems; rather these
would be institutions of academic excellence covering the full range
of instruction.

Kerr commented that many academicians consider urban and
community problems too low-ranking to be worthy of interest, while

they concentrate instead on national and international problems. He pointed out that involvement of these urban-grant universities in their cities would inevitably lead to controversy:

When you deal with urban problems, you deal with urban controversies and with urban politics. And so, for this university to work effectively, there will have to be a considerable amount of public understanding—especially understanding of the distinction between service based on application of knowledge and positions taken because of partisan politics (Kerr, 1968).

Kerr also argued that admissions standards should be lowered:

It might be desirable to adjust admissions standards somewhat to help make the urban-grant university more accessible to minority group students whose earlier educational experience may not have been completely adequate. I have a sense that faculty members across the country increasingly want to make a contribution to the problems of these students, and they feel they can. They certainly do not intend to lower the quality of the final product that comes out of the college. Rather by greater attention and greater concern, they intend to help make up the deficienc ies of the earlier years (ibid.).

Gerald Leinwand, chairman of the department of Education at the Bernard M. Baruch College of the City University of New York, argues for the creation of colleges of public education and service, writing in *Urban Review* (published by the Center for Urban Education) in 1969. Such colleges would replace the traditional teachers' colleges. They would be single-purpose institutions training professionals for public service only and would provide education for all who want to enter public service—professional and subprofessional alike. Public education and service colleges would have close ties to their communities, serving them as the communities wanted to be served. Such institutions would build their educational process around field experience in an urban setting. They would also be open to all who wish to enter.

INTERNAL REFORM Michael Rossman, a former student leader of the Free Speech Movement on the Berkeley campus in 1964, presents his position in a paper entitled *On Learning and Social Change* prepared for the Center for Educational Reform of the National Student Association. The university fails, says Rossman, not because it does research on the wrong things or because it is afraid to get involved, but because it does a poor job of teaching and is a poor place for people to spend time. The university does not provide a creative environment and is thus a poor educator. Rossman would do away with authority-centered learning, which he sees as a part of the authority complex of our culture. Instead he favors autonomous learning, which would allow people to realize their full potential for learning. "Our culture's central failure is its inability to help its people and itself learn how to learn."

Rossman describes the authority model of learning quite graphically as one in which "the expert produces knowledge, the teacher owns it and transmits it, and the pupil absorbs it." In this setting the teacher becomes an authority figure. Knowledge-centered learning would be built around flexible and partial forms of leadership rather than the rigid authority that now exists.

LIMITED INVOLVEMENT Roger Heyns, head of the American Council on Education and former chancellor of the University of California, Berkeley, attempts to define some criteria by which a university could determine whether it should become involved, in an article included in *Colleges and Universities as Agents of Social Change* (1968):

In general we have asked ourselves the following questions before deciding to go ahead:

(1) Can anyone else do it better?

(2) Is there a body of content, a discipline to be learned?

(3) Does the program draw on, as well as enrich, other programs?

All, again, educational questions (Heyns, p. 35).

Heyns also cites four lessons that he learned when the University of Michigan tried to be of service to the state of Michigan:

1 To obtain optimum results, the university must have a great deal of control of the field situation. The students must be geared into the agency to be sure that they aren't just additional manpower, or given routine assignments; real opportunities for learning must be provided. . . .

2 Nonetheless, by and large, we have not found it worthwhile to operate the field agency ourselves. Universities have pretty much abandoned their own elementary and secondary laboratory schools. We have greatly increased our use of regular hospitals for medical education as opposed to developing our own. . . . We are not in the business of operating social agencies. . . .

One little noticed but very real objection to university-operated and university-run social agencies [is that] the autonomy of the community itself may be compromised. We should be just as sensitive to the ability of the community to determine the kind of services it wants as we are to protecting our own freedom.

3   The practical learning experience must be related to the on-campus learning. The relation between theory and practice is complicated and great attention must be given to the complexities. The classroom learning must inform practice and vice versa. Mere uninterrupted experience is not enough.

4   The guiding concept for student behavior and experience is that he is a student — not a general citizen, not another member of the troops, and not an employee (Heyns, 1968, pp. 35–36).

Heyns concludes:

What about strictly service activities? These haven't been many and properly so. I think this is primarily because of the application of these criteria. We have not been, and we should not be, service stations. We have generally tried to select those service activities which are subject to our controls, those which met the requirements of the academy, and which contributed to the educational functions (Heyns, 1968, pp. 35–36).

The person who is accused of suggesting that universities retreat to the ivory tower is Jacques Barzun, historian, university administrator, and commentator on higher education. His critics misread his book *The American University* (1968) when they claim that it is against involvement. What Barzun says is that the university as we know it today is a delicate institution of recent creation whose central purpose is education. Service obligations cannot be permitted to disrupt this central function. One of Barzun's principal themes is that the services a university must render to its own students and faculty simply to be able to continue the process of education have put a tremendous strain on the university. It cannot be all things to all men. The faculty must devote its primary allegiance to teaching and to students.

Barzun notes that the number of claims on the university is unlimited, and those that lead to fragmentation must be resisted. Obviously the university must respond to many claims. However, its posture and method of response are critical. The university is not a business enterprise seeking to maximize its profit. But in a certain sense it is analogous to one. Most business enterprises specialize in a limited number of functions and do not attempt to go beyond their field of expertise. Faced with requests for assistance, Barzun says,

> . . . the university must make up its mind and choose between two attitudes which go with two messages incessantly heard. One is: "Behold our eminence—it deserves your support and affectionate regard after you have attended and shared our greatness." The other is: "We are a public utility like any other—drop in any time." Both messages are spoken by the same voice and both, perhaps, should remain unspoken, but the first should secretly inspire the "university conceived." Let it be clear: the choice is not between being high-hat and being just folks. It is not a question of hospitableness—a university should be hospitable; it is a question of style, reflecting the fundamental choice as to what the university thinks it is (Barzun, 1968, p. 285).

Barzun agrees with almost all other students of higher education that the principal purposes of universities should be teaching and research. One of the fundamental ways in which the university can increase its service is by making its education more widely available. Barzun is against elitism; those denied access can naturally be expected to be envious. "The remedy against the growth of envy is educational opportunity. The chance to learn is in theory denied to no one, and in practice it is being steadily enlarged" (Barzun, 1968, p. 248).

Just as Barzun claims that universities should be selective about the merit and the educational relevance of the requests made of them, he feels that there is great need for institutional reform. He is against overspecialization. He feels that the number of courses offered should be cut and the quality of those that remain raised. He favors better use of teachers' time and more independent study so that instructors do not simply recite what is contained in books. His concern is to make universities do a better job of teaching more people. Any reading of this as a call for retreat to the ivory tower is incorrect.

The authors cited have espoused four different positions that have a number of points in common. All agree that the primary goal of institutions of higher education is education. None claims that the university should become an all-purpose facility offering whatever service can make a profit for it. Barzun and Gardner do not occupy polar positions. Both agree that the university should do a better job of what it attempts. Gardner requests that a stronger effort be made and Barzun points out the pitfalls. An indication of the congruence of their positions is the fact that Barzun's book *The American University* (1968) (actually written before the Columbia revolution) is dedicated to John Gardner "In friendship and admiration."

References

Barzun, Jacques: *The American University: How It Runs, Where It Is Going,* Harper and Row, Publishers, Incorporated, New York, 1968.

Birenbaum, William M.: *Overlive: Power, Poverty, and the University,* Delacorte Press, Dell Publishing Co., Inc., New York, 1968.

Birenbaum, William M.: "Segregation and the Abuse of Due Process on the Campus," *Junior College Journal,* vol. 39, pp. 27–30, April 1969.

Gardner, John W.: *Excellence: Can We Be Equal and Excellent Too?* Harper and Row, Publishers, New York, 1961.

Gardner, John W.: "The Universities and the Cities," in John Caffrey. (ed.), *The Future Academic Community: Continuity and Change,* American Council on Education, Washington, D.C., 1969.

Heyns, Roger W.: "The University as an Instrument of Social Action," in W. John Minter and Ian M. Thompson (eds.), *Colleges and Universities as Agents of Social Change,* Center for Research and Development in Higher Education, Berkeley, Calif., and Western Interstate Commission for Higher Education, Boulder, Colo., 1968.

Kerr, Clark: *The Urban-Grant University: A Model for the Future,* lecture delivered October 18, 1967 at the centennial meeting of the City College (Gamma) Chapter of Phi Beta Kappa, City College Papers no. 8, City College, New York, 1968.

Leinwand, Gerald: "Needed: A College of Public Education and Service," *Urban Review,* vol. 3, pp. 19–22, April 1969.

Rossman, Michael: *On Learning and Social Change,* National Student Association, Washington, D.C., n.d. (Mineographed.)

This book was set in Vladimir by University Graphics, Inc.
It was printed on acid-free, long-life paper and bound by
The Maple Press Company. The designers were Elliot Epstein
and Edward Butler. The editors were Nancy Tressel and
Michael Hennelly for McGraw-Hill Book Company and Verne A.
Stadtman and Sidney J. P. Hollister for the Carnegie Commission
on Higher Education. Joe Campanella supervised the production.